Welcome to AuDHD

Welcome to AuDHD

How to Survive (and Thrive) as an
Adult with Autism and ADHD

Megan Griffith

Jessica Kingsley Publishers
London and Philadelphia

First published in Great Britain in 2026 by Jessica Kingsley Publishers
An imprint of John Murray Press

7

A CIP catalogue record for this title is available from the British Library and the Library of Congress

ISBN 978 1 80501 238 2
eISBN 978 1 80501 239 9

Printed by Integrated Books International, United States of America

Jessica Kingsley Publishers' policy is to use papers that are natural, renewable and recyclable products and made from wood grown in sustainable forests. The logging and manufacturing processes are expected to conform to the environmental regulations of the country of origin.

Jessica Kingsley Publishers
Carmelite House
50 Victoria Embankment
London EC4Y 0DZ

www.jkp.com

John Murray Press
Part of Hodder & Stoughton Ltd
An Hachette Company

The authorised representative in the EEA is Hachette Ireland,
8 Castlecourt Centre, Dublin 15, D15 XTP3, Ireland (email: info@hbgi.ie)

To my husband.
Thank you for learning about AuDHD and talking about it with me endlessly, without letting it change how much we love each other. You are the best, and I love you.

Contents

Note on Language

Throughout this book, you may notice times where I address autism singularly or ADHD singularly, despite the fact that this is a book about the unique experience of being both.

This is because there are certain aspects of the AuDHD experience that are primarily shaped by either autism or ADHD, and I want to acknowledge where those particular aspects stem from.

For example, when I talk about difficulty with literal thinking, I will likely reference autism first and foremost. Don't worry, the way this autistic trait interacts with ADHD will also be addressed, but it's important to me to differentiate between primarily autistic traits and primarily ADHD traits, and then to explore how those traits interact.

Preface

Alright, so you're autistic and ADHD—AuDHD. And you're completely lost.

Maybe these diagnoses took you totally by surprise, or maybe you've been suspecting them for a while, but regardless, you're a little floored right now.

Because aren't autism and ADHD for kids? Aren't you supposed to grow out of them? Who ever heard of an adult diagnosed with autism and ADHD?

Yeah, don't feel bad for thinking this way. Our society absolutely paints autism and ADHD in that kind of light. A quick Google search for either "autism" or "ADHD" will generate results pretty much exclusively aimed at helping parents cope with kids who have these conditions.

Which leads to another pervasive story our society likes to tell about autism and ADHD: that we are burdens to be borne by others. For decades, autism and ADHD have been defined by how our conditions affect the people around us, rather than how they affect, well, *us*.

This book is the antidote to that kind of nonsense.

Because you are not a burden.

You are a light.

Think of this book as a disco ball, scattering your light everywhere, illuminating the parts of yourself that you've hidden away for years, in fear and shame. It's not my job to shine a light on your darkness, but rather to reflect your own light back to you so you can see how amazing you already are.

I know this whole AuDHD thing is a lot. Understanding yourself through this lens will change your life, in the most amazing way. It will be hard at times, and that's okay. It's hard work worth doing.

So, let's get started.

Before we dive in, I just want to take a moment to welcome you to the AuDHD family. If you're anything like me, you've felt like a bit of an outcast your whole life. You didn't fit in with the neuro-typicals, but your struggles weren't obvious enough to get you the help you needed, so for a long time, you lived in this liminal space where you were just...wrong. No matter what you did or said or felt, it was wrong. And there was no explanation for this wrongness, so you assumed it must be you. Who you were was simply wrong.

But this wasn't true, was it?

You were AuDHD all along. And you're finally in the place where you're right. Where everything about you fits just the way it should.

Welcome.

Part 1

Welcome to AuDHD

CHAPTER 1

What Is Autism, ADHD, and AuDHD?

It seems like most of us AuDHDers experience two key things after diagnosis (self or professional): validation and imposter syndrome.

At first, we're like, "Oh my God, of *course*. This explains literally everything."

But shortly thereafter, doubt starts creeping in. We pour over the diagnostic criteria for the millionth time, and we can't help but see all the ways we don't quite fit. And we start to wonder if we made things up or exaggerated, or if we'd just read and watched so much content about AuDHD that we convinced ourselves and/or our assessor that we're something we're not.

There's a couple of very good reasons we do this.

First, society has a very limited view of autism and ADHD. Both are expected to primarily affect children, especially white boys. We're not given an image of an AuDHD adult, a Black AuDHDer, a trans AuDHDer, or really any other intersectional identity. And as human beings, we often struggle to accept the parts of ourselves that we've never seen represented.

Second, many autistic folks think quite literally, and this absolutely applies to how we read the criteria for autism and ADHD.

We read the latest version of the *Diagnostic and Statistic Manual* (DSM-V-TR) and we can't help but notice that we don't do *exactly* what it's saying, and we wonder if we really fit.*

Third, the language in the DSM is cold, clinical, and highly deficits-based. For many autistic folks, this language suits us just fine because we better understand ourselves and the world through logic, and we don't see our deficits as anything to be ashamed of or resist. But for many other autistics, this language feels inhuman and shaming, and therefore it's hard to picture ourselves ever fully fitting into it.

Finally, those criteria were not written from the perspective of what it's like to actually be autistic or ADHD. They were written from the perspective of an exasperated teacher or parent or clinician who just wants to understand why a child is behaving this way. The criteria are highly behavioral, and almost entirely leave out the internal experience of autism and ADHD. And because we know both conditions are not behavioral, but neurodevelopmental, this is an inherently incomplete picture.

So, let's paint a new picture. One created by us, for us.

In the next pages, you'll find rewritten criteria for autism, ADHD, and AuDHD, based on both research and lived experience.

Highlight and annotate to your heart's content.

What is autism?

If you've been diagnosed as AuDHD, either self-diagnosed or professionally, you probably already know that autism is a

---

* The DSM is the *Diagnostic Statistical Manual*, a book full of all the diagnoses recognized by the American Psychiatric Association. For those not in the United States, the DSM may be used for diagnosis, but another common manual is the ICD, the *International Classification of Diseases*. See www.psychiatry.org/psychiatrists/practice/dsm/frequently-asked-questions

neurodevelopmental condition that affects how you process the world.

Okay, but like...what does that *mean*?

It means that your brain has developed differently, resulting in a processing style that differs from allistic (non-autistic) brains.

Because this isn't an academic or medical research text (and I'm not a psychiatrist or any other kind of doctor), we won't do too deep a dive into the anatomical and functional differences in the autistic brain. Instead, we'll focus on the resulting processing style.

Autism affects your cognitive, sensory, emotional, and social processing, and it also affects how all those things interact with one another.

So, let's explore the differences in how autistics interpret input, how this results in different output, and how these differences lead to disability.

Input

This is a completely different way of processing sensory, emotional, cognitive, and social input when compared to neurotypical processing.

The sensory-emotional-cognitive connection

Neurotypical folks experience a distinct separation between sensory, emotional, and cognitive experiences with occasional overflow from one category to the next, but autistic folks experience overflow on a regular basis. An intense sensory experience can produce or contribute to an intense emotional experience, a difficult cognitive problem can increase sensory difficulty, and so on and so forth. All of these can combine to affect social processing as well.

Sensory processing

Hyper- and/or hyposensitivity: Very few autistics experience only hypersensitivity or only hyposensitivity; we generally experience a unique mix of over- and undersensitivity to a variety of inputs. For example, the same autistic person might simultaneously experience hypersensitivity to light touch and hyposensitivity to pain. Hyper- or hyposensitivity can happen in any of the senses:

- sight
- sound
- touch
- smell
- taste
- proprioception (awareness of your body in space)
- vestibular (sense of balance)
- interoception (awareness of your internal experiences, such as hunger cues, temperature awareness, and more).

Lack of habituation: Autistic folks rarely experience something called habituation,[1] the phenomenon where we gradually ignore repetitive experiences. For example, an autistic person may have difficulty tuning out the tinny, high-pitched sound of electricity because they don't habituate.

Emotional processing

Alexithymia: Autistic folks are significantly more likely than neurotypical folks to experience alexithymia,[2] difficulty identifying emotions while they're occurring.

Hyper- and/or hyposensitivity: Just like with sensory processing, many autistic folks are either hyper- or hyposensitive to emotional experiences, and this can vary within each individual person. For example, some autistic folks are always very sensitive (many autistic folks identify as a Highly Sensitive Person[3] before realizing they are autistic), others always experience life without significant emotional input, and others may experience both extremes in different situations.

Emotional dysregulation: Many autistic folks struggle with emotional regulation.[4] This can look like intense mood swings and strong, seemingly inappropriate emotional reactions (that are in-fact often very appropriate for what's happening internally).

Cognitive processing

Attention to detail and cognitive overload: Many autistic folks have extraordinary attention to detail.[5] We can't help but notice every little detail about everything, which can lead to cognitive overwhelm.

Rigid thinking patterns: Many autistic folks experience very rigid thinking patterns. This may look like black-and-white thinking, obsessive tendencies, highly literal thinking or highly metaphorical thinking, and/or compulsive thinking patterns.

Social processing

Hyper- and/or hyposensitivity: As with sensory and emotional input, autistics often experience hyper- or hyposensitivity to social input. Hyper- and hyposensitivity can co-exist in the same person in different contexts. For example, an autistic person may be hyposensitive to facial expressions, as in they simply do not notice changes in facial expressions or the meaning behind them, but also be hypersensitive to social hierarchies and immediately pinpoint who's in charge in any given group. Additionally, someone who is naturally hyposensitive to social input may develop very concentrated, intentional hypersensitivity to social input as a way to cope. For instance, if someone consistently gets in trouble for making social faux pas, they might learn to study and memorize various social cues to hide their natural social processing style.

Output

This different way of processing then produces very different behavioral output when compared to neurotypical behavior.

Non-speaking

Many, though not all, autistics are non-speaking to some degree. Previously described as nonverbal, many autistics prefer the term "non-speaking" because lack of speech does not indicate lack of verbal understanding or ability to communicate in words in other ways, such as AAC (alternative and augmentative communication). Some autistic folks are entirely non-speaking; others are non-speaking on an episodic basis, often called "verbal shutdowns". Many people who experience verbal shutdowns experience them in periods of burnout or high stress, be that emotional, cognitive, or sensory stress.

Stimming

All human beings engage in something called self-stimulatory behavior, AKA stimming. But autistic folks often engage in more frequent and more obvious stimming, such as hand flapping, hair twirling, jumping, spinning, and so much more, and this stimming may relieve sensory, emotional, or cognitive stress.

Meltdowns and shutdowns

Many autistic folks experience meltdowns, shutdowns, or both.

Meltdowns are intense and uncontrollable experiences that may affect emotions, cognition, and/or sensory processing.[6] Basically, the nervous system says, "Nope, this is absolutely too much to handle, we cannot do this." From there, people often react in one of three ways: externalizing, internalizing, or shutting down.

- **Externalized meltdowns** are what you might consider "classic" meltdowns. An externalized meltdown is when an autistic person finds a way to outwardly express their distress through hitting things, shouting, running away (AKA eloping), and/or other outward behaviors.

- **Internalized meltdowns** might look mild on the outside (crying, pacing, staring into space, etc.), but they are just as chaotic and distressing as an externalized meltdown. Internally, the autistic person may be experiencing intense negative self-talk, spiraling or racing thoughts, or even suicidal ideation.

- **Shutdowns**, on the other hand, happen when the nervous system has the opposite reaction.[7] Instead of turning the dial up to 11, it gets shut off entirely. Externally, this may look like flat affect (no facial expression and monotone voice), being unable or unwilling to speak, intense fatigue, or staring into space. Internally, this experience is highly dissociative. The autistic person experiencing a shutdown is likely completely out of touch with their own emotions, thoughts, and body.

Special interests

Due to our rigid thinking, many autistic folks experience something typically referred to as "special interests." Some people prefer terms like "specialized knowledge" or "areas of expertise," but regardless of the label, special interests are areas where the autistic person is essentially an expert due to months—and more often, years—of intensive research and immersion into the topic. Literally anything can become a special interest, from psychology (one of my special interests) to insects to ABBA. Special interests often span a lifetime, but they certainly don't have to. Many autistic folks experience special interests for months at a time, and then they slip away or morph into something else. If you've experienced what felt like a special interest for just a few weeks, there's a good chance your experience is best described as an ADHD hyperfixation, which we'll get into when we discuss the modified ADHD criteria.

Hyper- or hypoexpressive facial expressions and body language

Many autistic folks demonstrate either hyper- or hypoexpressive facial expressions and body language. Just as with hyper- and hyposensitivity, these can co-exist in one person in various contexts. Sometimes an autistic person's hyperexpressive facial expressions and body language are natural, and other times they are practiced—a way of trying to appear more neurotypical by being more expressive than they would naturally be. Many autistic people actually practice their facial expressions in the mirror in an effort to appear more neurotypical.

Routines and resistance to change

Due to rigid thinking patterns and existence in a society that does not prioritize the accommodation of autistic people's needs, many autistic folks follow a strict routine and have a lot of trouble with change. It's hard to adapt to changed plans when you're not sure if the new plans will suit your sensory, emotional, cognitive, or social needs, and it's often far more comfortable for autistic folks to do something the same way every time. This might involve taking a shower the exact same way every time or eating the exact same food for lunch every day.

Masking

Many autistic folks consciously and subconsciously hide their autistic traits through masking,[8] an exhausting performance of neurotypicality meant to keep the autistic person safe in social situations where they might be ridiculed, abused, or even killed for their autistic traits.[9] Masking can look like forcing eye contact even if it feels uncomfortable, suppressing stims, mimicking the facial expressions of others, and more.

Disability

This combination of different input processing and different behavioral output often leads to disability. In some ways, this disability is due to a world that prioritizes the neurotypical experience, and if society changed to be more inclusive, much of that disability would disappear, but there are also some inherently disabling traits of autism that cannot be accommodated socially and, regardless of accommodation, lead to very real, unavoidable limitations. More on autism as a disability in Chapter 7: Disability Is Not a Dirty Word.

What is ADHD?

As many folks have been saying for years, attention-deficit hyperactivity disorder (ADHD) is one of the worst-named conditions in the DSM. ADHD is so much more than a deficit in attention. Sure, often we struggle to pay attention, but other times, we may struggle to stop paying attention, and a lot of ADHDers experience struggles outside of attention, often called executive dysfunction.

Executive functioning is a lot of things, but generally speaking, it's the ability to make executive decisions. This includes decisions about what you want to focus on, what you want to think about, and how you want to spend your time. When you experience executive dysfunction, you often feel like you're not the one in charge of your brain. Like things just...happen to you. And you're left in a state of constantly reacting to life instead of actively living your life.

Okay, this sounds eerily familiar. So, what is executive functioning exactly?

There are actually all kinds of different executive functions. Some sources say there are seven, or 11, or even 12, but for the purposes of this book, we'll explore eight primary types of executive dysfunction:[10]

- **Impulse control:** The ability to experience urges and impulses and make active decisions about whether or not to act on them.
  When we struggle: Impulsivity or inhibition.

- **Emotional regulation:** The ability to feel your feelings fully and then return to a relatively stable baseline.
  When we struggle: Mood swings, chronic numbness, rejection sensitivity.

- **Task initiation:** The ability to identify a task that needs to be completed, then begin working on that task with relative ease.
  When we struggle: Difficulty getting started, "wasting" time, long transition periods between tasks.

- **Working memory:** The ability to hold information in your mind while working with other information.
  When we struggle: Forgetfulness.

- **Flexible thinking:** The ability to adjust your thinking based on context or new information.
  When we struggle: Black-and-white thinking, rigid thinking, difficulty with change.

- **Self-monitoring:** The ability to perceive yourself and your behavior and make sense of it.
  When we struggle: Lack of sense of self or lack of self-awareness.

- **Planning and prioritization:** The ability to make active decisions about what is more or less important, urgent, or time-sensitive.
  When we struggle: Trying to do everything at once or doing things in an unhelpful order.

- **Organization:** The ability to categorize things in a helpful way.
  When we struggle: Doom piles, "scatterbrained," ADHD paralysis.

Notice how none of these are really about not paying enough attention—at least, not solely that. Seriously, ADHD is very poorly named. It's one reason why so many people go undiagnosed for so long, because they can pay attention when they really have to. All the other issues in their lives, like a painfully messy house, endless late fees, or taking forever to get shit done, gets written off as "laziness," when in reality, laziness doesn't even exist.[11]

I see you, reading that last sentence over, wondering if you've misunderstood, or maybe scoffing at my naiveté. But according to Devon Price, social psychologist and author of both *Laziness Does Not Exist* and *Unmasking Autism*, laziness truly doesn't exist. It's always something else.

Burnout. Self-care. Depression. And yes, executive dysfunction.

So, if ADHD isn't laziness and it isn't a lack of attention, what is it exactly? Just like autism, it's a neurodevelopmental disability, and the DSM criteria are based much more on how hyperactive little boys interrupted their teachers' lectures than how ADHD actually feels, especially at the intersection of identities other than young, white, cis boys.

Let's take a look at my new, revised ADHD criteria, written by an ADHDer, for ADHDers.

Input

A completely different way of perceiving cognitive, emotional, sensory, and social input when compared to a neurotypical processing style.

No input filter

Folks with ADHD do not have much in the way of an input filter. Many neurotypicals automatically and subconsciously sort through input and decide what's relevant and what's irrelevant, but ADHDers experience all input simultaneously, at the same level of relevance.[12] This can lead to a sense of overwhelm and increase hyperactivity, as there is so much to pay attention to and think about/act on.

Rejection Sensitive Dysphoria

Many ADHDers interpret neutral input as negative[13] which can lead to feelings of rejection even when it's not actually present, resulting in Rejection Sensitive Dysphoria (RSD). There is much debate about whether RSD is an inherent trait of ADHD or a learned trauma response to the actual increased rejection experienced by many ADHDers (discussed in more depth in the "Output" section of these redefined criteria).

Boredom

Studies show that ADHD is closely correlated with increased susceptibility to boredom,[14] which many ADHDers describe as mentally painful. Boredom for us is not apathy or mindlessness—it's actually the opposite. It's painful mindfulness. We're so aware of everything happening at once (see "No input filter" above) that we have trouble focusing on any one thing, leading us to feel intensely bored, even when surrounded by stimulation that non-ADHDers might find interesting or engaging.

Emotional dysregulation

As with autism, emotional dysregulation is a significant part of the ADHD experience.[15] This can look like quick and seemingly disproportionate emotional reactions to situations, with difficulty returning to baseline.

Increased habituation

Unlike autism, which tends to come with a lack of habituation, ADHDers often habituate to things much more quickly than neurotypical folks.[16] This is one reason that rewards are typically effective for a much shorter time with ADHD: because the reward quickly no longer feels "special," but rather feels normal, because we've habituated to it. This is directly related to our ADHD need for novelty. We're always chasing that next interesting thing, because when we're exposed to something repeatedly, we start to tune it out, leaving us without the stimulation we need.

Hyperfocus

Despite all the input ADHDers are constantly trying to process at the same time, which often leads to distractability, sometimes the opposite happens and we hyperfocus.[17] This looks like a long-lasting episode (often hours) of engaging with one specific thing and ignoring everything else, sometimes including eating, drinking, or even using the bathroom. There are some positive features of hyperfocus, like being able to get things done, which many ADHDers often struggle with, but it can also be frustrating because it could lead to missing important deadlines or appointments or making yourself sick due to not being aware of your body's cues for hunger, thirst, or relief.

Output

This different way of processing then produces very different behavioral output when compared to neurotypical behavior:

Inattentive

Some of the ways that ADHD affects our output are inattentive in nature, including the following:

- **Difficulty working with minutiae:** Many ADHDers struggle to do things like pay attention to grammar, fill in every single box on forms, or do minor calculations correctly.[18] Contrary to popular belief, this is not due to a lack of care, but rather due to overwhelm associated with the "no input filter" and "boredom" discussed above. In order to avoid the mental pain of overwhelm and boredom, we often avoid minutiae entirely, or deal with them as quickly as we can, without double-checking our work.

- **Difficulty starting tasks:** One of the executive functions listed above is "task initiation," and because ADHD is an executive functioning condition, it comes as no surprise that we tend to struggle to initiate tasks.[19] We might work on something else as a way of avoiding the task at hand, or we might get stuck doom-scrolling on our phones, desperately wishing we could be doing what we want to do, but nonetheless feeling totally trapped by our inability to start.

- **Frequent task switching:** Despite the fact that the research shows that ADHDers tend to expend more energy on switching tasks than non-ADHDers,[20] we also tend to do it more often due to difficulty with sustained attention. This basically means that we struggle to keep our attention focused on one thing for very long. For example, I have stopped writing mid-sentence to check something countless times already while writing this book.

- **Difficulty finishing tasks:** This trouble with sustained attention can also cause us to have a really hard time finishing anything. The entire task completion process is often a nightmare for ADHDers. It's nearly impossible to get ourselves to start anything, and once we do, it's nearly impossible to actually pay attention to that task, which then makes it nearly impossible to ever finish that task.

- **Misperception of time:** Many ADHDers completely misperceive the passage of time.[21] This can look like working on something, glancing at the clock, which says 2pm, then going back to work, only to glance at the clock five minutes later and have it say 5:30pm. This often leads to lateness and something the community likes to call "waiting mode." This is when, in an effort not to misperceive time and miss something, we feel we can't start anything several hours before a meeting, event, or appointment. We may literally stare at the wall for hours, trying to be productive in some small way, but totally unable to.

- **Lack of environmental awareness:** If you've ever been called a "space cadet," you get this one. ADHDers are usually less aware of their surroundings than non-ADHDers, leading to issues like appearing to ignore people speaking directly to you, increased car accidents,[22] and "zoning out" frequently.

- **Losing things:** Many ADHDers lose things on a regular basis.[23] This is sometimes due to a lack of attention paid when setting down or putting away the object; other times, we lose things because of the mental load of keeping track of too many things. Basically, we just can't keep track of it all, so some information gets tossed.

Hyperactive

Some of the ways that ADHD affects our output are hyperactive in nature, including the following:

- **Fidgeting:** One way hyperactivity can manifest outwardly in ADHD is fidgeting. Unlike fidgeting in folks without ADHD, which is often a sign of anxiety or a way of distracting your-self, fidgeting in ADHD often helps us focus more, not less, and may be completely removed from anxiety.[24] Common fidgets include knee bouncing, pen clicking, hand wringing, foot tapping, pacing, or playing with toys specifically made for fidgeting, like fidget spinners, tangles, or fidget rings.

- **Interrupting:** Hyperactivity in ADHD is often seen in the way that ADHDers tend to interrupt others, not out of rudeness, but due to issues with both impulse control and working memory. What happens is, we have a thought that we'd like to share, but based on past experience, we know that if we don't share that thought quickly, we'll forget it. So we feel increased pressure to share, and due to impulse control issues, we can't hold ourselves back for long and we end up interrupting others.

- **Hyperfixations:** A hyperfixation is an intense interest that lasts longer than a day or two, but often isn't quite as long-lasting as an autistic special interest. A lot of ADHDers get stuck on their interests for days, weeks, or even months at a time. We become completely consumed by whatever it is we're into lately, only for that passion to slowly peter out or, sometimes, suddenly disappear without warning.

- **Difficulty processing energy:** You know how some people are lactose intolerant, and their bodies simply can't prop-erly process dairy? ADHDers are kind of like that, but with energy. We can't process it in a way that's useful for us, either internally or externally. Here's what I mean by that:

  - **Internal:** Studies show that ADHDers experience a higher sense of internal restlessness compared to non-ADHDers.[25] We all have an internal sense of energy, but for those of us with ADHD, that internal energy is often chaotic, unpredictable, and switches rapidly (likely due to the lack of an input filter previously discussed). It can often feel like our energy and our intentions are at war with each other and the energy is impossible to wrangle and point in one particular direction for any sustained amount of time.

- **External:** Though I have a lot of problems with the original DSM-V criteria for ADHD, I do very much like where they used the phrase "driven by a motor."[26] ADHD energy processing difficulties can absolutely result in us feeling and acting as if we're being driven by a motor. More specifically, like a car with a brick on the gas pedal. We can't really seem to stop, even when we'd like to. This can look like having tons of ideas flow through our heads all at once, running around the house like a chicken with our heads cut off, trying to get things done, and scheduling our day so that it's so packed that there's literally no downtime at all.

Compensation

Some ADHDers might feel that they relate to the "Input" section of these criteria, but relate to very little of the "Output" section. This is often largely due to compensation behaviors.[27] For example, you might compensate for difficulty finishing tasks by giving yourself much more time than non-ADHDers to get things done. Or you might not be a big fidgeter, but maybe you exercise and go for a walk and pace around your house every single day. These compensatory behaviors might decrease symptoms/traits (explaining why so many ADHDers fly under the radar for so long), but they still take up a lot of time, energy, and focus, which non-ADHDers do not have to expend.

Disability

This combination of different input processing and different behavioral output often leads to disability. In some ways, this disability is due to a world that prioritizes the neurotypical experience, and if society changed to be more inclusive, much of that disability would disappear, but there are also some inherently disabling traits of ADHD that cannot be accommodated socially and, regardless of accommodation, lead to very real, unavoidable limitations. More on ADHD as a disability in Chapter 7: Disability Is Not a Dirty Word.

So...what about AuDHD?

The thing is, you can look at these criteria all day, but if you have both autism and ADHD, it's going to look different. They play off each other, mask each other, exacerbate each other, and so much more.

Being AuDHD is incredibly different from being solely autistic or being solely ADHD.

So, let's break down the input, output, and disability of AuDHD specifically.

Input

This is a completely different way of perceiving cognitive, emotional, sensory, and social input when compared to a neurotypical processing style.

Inconsistent sleep needs

Generally speaking, most adults need at least seven hours of sleep each night, and young adults or folks recovering from illness or sleep debt (getting less than seven hours of sleep on a regular or semi-regular basis) may benefit from nine or more hours of sleep each night.[28] However, many AuDHDers may swing back and forth between needing well over nine hours of sleep in a night to needing far less than seven hours. This inconsistency reflects a general pattern you will likely notice as I describe what it's like to be AuDHD, which is that we tend to struggle with regulation or finding any kind of middle ground.

Additionally, studies show that those of us with autism and/or ADHD are more likely to deal with something called delayed sleep-wake phase disorder,[29] which is a condition where we produce melatonin (the sleepy time hormone) much later in the day than most folks, which means it's much harder for us to fall asleep around 10–11pm, and we are more likely to only get sleepy once it hits 2–3am. This obviously makes it hard to get enough sleep, since most schools and jobs require us to be awake anywhere from 5am to 7am.

Emotional dysregulation

I've mentioned this in both the autism and ADHD sections, but it bears repeating. Many AuDHDers experience such extreme emotional dysregulation that many of us are misdiagnosed with bipolar disorder before we realize we are actually autistic[30] and ADHD[31] (to be fair, many of us actually do have bipolar in addition to our AuDHD, but bipolar alone does not explain our experiences).

Narrow window of tolerance

Many AuDHDers experience something called a narrow window of tolerance, which basically means that we are both easily overstimulated and easily understimulated.

We need a very precise amount of stimulation to feel comfortable in our own skin.

Overstimulation is most commonly caused by autistic sensory sensitivities, though it could also be triggered by the internal hyperactivity of ADHD (sometimes the volume and velocity of our own thoughts can overwhelm us). This typically feels like extreme discomfort. Everything just feels...wrong. Your skin is itchy, you can't focus on anything anyone is saying, you're weirdly aware of how big your tongue is in your mouth, and you have a strong urge to leave this overstimulating situation.

Understimulation is most commonly caused by the ADHD need for more stimulation than a non-ADHDer,[32] though it could also be triggered by the autistic need for stimulation in order to self-regulate (especially if you're more on the sensory-seeking end of the spectrum). This, too, feels like everything is utterly wrong. But instead of everything feeling like too much, it feels like you're looking for something...but you don't know what. You might wander your house trying different things: drink some water, eat a snack, scroll social media, turn on a comfort show, but none of it is *right*.

If you're both autistic and ADHD and you are prone to both over- and understimulation, it can feel impossible to actually be comfortable. It's a precarious game, seeking stimulation, but not too much, and of course it has to be the right kind of stimulation in order to really scratch that itch.

Output

This different way of processing then produces very different behavioral output when compared to neurotypical behavior:

Teacher's Pet, Class Clown, or "Problem Child"

Many AuDHDers take on very specific roles in the classroom

growing up, probably because our autistic brain doesn't instinctually understand social dynamics, and so it tries to use shortcuts like playing a part. Oh, and because when we actually act like ourselves, we're often met with blank stares.

Some AuDHDers may take on the role of Teacher's Pet, finding security through being liked and approved of by an authority figure. We don't understand all the social rules, but for the most part, we understand the rules about how we're expected to behave. So we follow them to the letter.

Other AuDHDers may be more of a Class Clown, using humor to distract from our near-constant discomfort and confusion. If everyone was laughing *with* us, they couldn't laugh *at* us. Plus, for many folks with ADHD, our impulsivity can make us genuinely good at improv. And let's be honest, it just felt nice to be good at something for a change.

Finally, some AuDHDers are labeled the "Problem Child," and even if we try to resist at first, most of us eventually give in to the label because nothing we do seems to persuade anyone to think any differently. These are often the AuDHDers who struggle to hide our traits and symptoms, or whose traits and symptoms present in ways that are more inconvenient for the authority figures in our lives. We might have frequent meltdowns, question authority, self-medicate with substances, or be wholly apathetic, having given up on ourselves.

"But you're so normal!"

So many of us, when we finally realize we're AuDHD, hear this constant refrain from our friends and family. Why? Why do they think we're so "normal" when we've spent our whole lives struggling?

Well, autism and ADHD can sometimes mask each other. Got caught daydreaming in class? Good thing the unit this week is on your special interest and you already know pretty much everything about it. Had a meltdown last night where you were close to self-harming? No worries, thanks to your ADHD tendency to think of time in terms of "now" or "not now," it feels like eons ago and you act totally normal at school the next day.

From the outside, AuDHDers sometimes (though of course not always) behave much like a neurotypical person. It just involves a lot more effort than it does for neurotypical folks.

Self-medicating

Studies have long shown that ADHD is associated with increased risk of substance use disorder,[33] but more recent studies show that the combination of ADHD and autism is also highly linked with substance use disorders and increased vulnerability to dependence.[34]

Understanding the reason behind this connection is complicated and probably has a lot to do with neurology, but if I had to hazard a guess, it probably also has something to do with how overwhelming the world is and how substances often numb some of that. It's probably related to how uncomfortable we are in social situations and the fact that substances are often used as a social lubricant. And it almost definitely has to do with our ongoing identity crisis caused by masking.

Disability

This combination of different input processing and different behavioral output often leads to disability. In some ways, this disability is due to a world that prioritizes the neurotypical experience, and if society changed to be more inclusive, much of that disability would disappear, but there are also some inherently disabling traits of being AuDHD that cannot be accommodated socially and, regardless of accommodation, lead to very real, unavoidable limitations. More on AuDHD as a disability in Chapter 7: Disability Is Not a Dirty Word.

Alright, so we know what we're dealing with now, through the lens of what it's like to actually *be* AuDHD, rather than what it's like to be inconvenienced by us. And reading all that, you might be thinking, "Wow, this chick really knows her stuff, she must've been diagnosed as a kid and spent her whole life learning about all this."

Well, you'd be wrong.

I actually received my autism and ADHD diagnoses in 2022, at the age of 27. And I happen to know that my story of flying under the radar is a very common one.

So, let's talk about it.

KEY TAKEAWAYS

➜ Being AuDHD looks totally different from being solely autistic or solely ADHD.

➜ Autism and ADHD are both neurodevelopmental disabilities, *not* behavioral disorders, and as such, autism and ADHD can manifest both externally *and* internally.

➜ The DSM, while a useful tool in many ways, was primarily written from the perspective of how autistic and ADHD children inconvenienced the adults around them, and therefore it's highly deficits-based and is not really written with adults in mind.

limitations. More on AuDHD as a disability in Chapter 7, Disability
Is Not a Dirty Word.

Alright, so we know what we're dealing with now. Through the
lens of what it's like to actually be AuDHD, rather than what it's
like to be inconvenienced by us. And reading all of this, you might
be thinking, "Wow, this chick really knows her stuff, she must've
been diagnosed—"

Well, you'd be wrong.

I actually received my autism and ADHD diagnoses in 2023, at
the age of 22. And I happen to know that my story of living under
the radar is a very common one.

So, let's talk about it.

CHAPTER 2
Making Sense of Who You Are

I am professionally diagnosed as both autistic and ADHD.

But before that, I was self-diagnosed. And before that, I was misdiagnosed. And before *that*, I was suppressing literally everything, pretending I was fine so that I could survive.

No matter where you are on your journey exploring your AuDHD self, this chapter will guide you toward understanding and acceptance.

Not sure if self-diagnosis "counts"? We'll address that.

Already got diagnosed with either autism or ADHD, but can't convince a professional to diagnose you with the other one? We'll discuss how to talk to professionals so that they listen.

Don't have a freaking clue how you're supposed to just...live your normal life, having had your entire self-concept turned upside down? Yeah, we'll dig into that too.

My journey to AuDHD

"S top being so dramatic" was the refrain of my childhood.

It seems that no one could wrap their brains around a seven-year-old who contemplated death through Barbie funerals and sang to her strawberry plant and was afraid of everything from putting in contacts to swallowing pills.

I just didn't make sense to the people in my life. They loved me deeply, but they didn't understand me. And they knew it. And this knowing led to an intense fear: that others wouldn't understand me either, and because they didn't already love me, their lack of understanding would lead to bullying.

My parents were terrified of me getting bullied. Because even if they didn't understand my sensitivity, they saw it. And they knew others would see it too, and the others might not be so kind because I wasn't their kid. I would just be an easy target.

As far as I know, I was never bullied in school, but fun fact: a lot of autistic folks don't always realize when we're being bullied. We think people are laughing *with* us, when really they're laughing *at* us. I suppose I might have been teased, but I'm fairly certain I never experienced true bullying. And I know it's at least in part because of that refrain: "Stop being so dramatic." So, even though I felt very invalidated by it, in some ways I'm thankful I was trained to be less dramatic, at least on the outside.

But internally, I remained as dramatic, sensitive, and obsessive as ever. Maybe more so, because I had no outlet for it. Instead, I tried to banish that dramatic part of me, and in its place, growing deep in my subconscious, was shame.

So many AuDHDers grow up to be ashamed of themselves for expressing traits that are so wholeheartedly othered in our society that we don't just feel "different" or "odd," but we also feel "alien" and "wrong."

Like who we are is a mistake we must always be trying to fix.

And a person can only live their life believing they are a mistake for so long before they snap.

I lost it in college, as so many of us do, with the decreased support and increased responsibilities that push our limited capacities to their breaking points.

When I first sought therapy, I was diagnosed with bipolar

disorder, which is actually a very common misdiagnosis for both ADHD[1] and autism.[2]

That diagnosis made sense to me, at first. I had spent so many years repressing my sensitivity that I no longer saw any correlation between my emotions and the things that caused them. My moods felt random, which to my knowledge, back then, felt in line with bipolar.

But as the years went on and I did more and more research, I started to know, deep in my bones, that I wasn't bipolar. This wasn't right. I didn't really fit. My "mania" was too mild, even for "hypomania." My cycles were too quick, even for "ultra rapid cycling bipolar." I doubted and doubted and doubted, and then I started working with a trauma therapist who helped me see how repressing my sensitivity absolutely "counted" as trauma.

The floodgates opened. I realized all those "random" mood swings weren't random at all—they were triggers. I was trying so hard to keep repressing my sensitivity, but it was leaking out everywhere, and all I was gaining by trying to suppress it was confusion about what was going on.

I wasn't bipolar. My therapist agreed. I was traumatized.

For a while, I thought that was it.

But a few things just weren't right.

First off, my siblings aren't like me. They don't act traumatized. And we've had many discussions about how my perception of our childhood just doesn't fit with theirs. They didn't see all the invalidation over my sensitivity that I am sure I experienced.

Second, I wasn't being invalidated because my loved ones were jerks. I was being invalidated because I had an inherently different experience from them that they did not understand.

So, what caused that inherently different experience?

A few years ago, deep into the pandemic, riddled with a seemingly never-ending obsession with my mental health, I started to find the answers. On TikTok.

After I saw and liked my first autism TikTok, it only took a few days for my FYP to be positively flooded with autistic content. And it made my whole life make sense in a way it never had before. Not with the bipolar or the trauma or anything else.

I started doing research beyond TikTok, reading as many books and articles as I could, and within six months of seeing that first TikTok, I decided to self-diagnose.

I was autistic. Finally, the world made sense. *I* made sense.

But then I had a therapist and a psychiatrist both dismiss me, emphatically certain that I couldn't be autistic. I was shattered, but I so badly wanted to understand myself, and they were the experts, so I took it all back.

I had announced my self-diagnosis online, so I felt compelled to announce my un-diagnosis online, embarrassed and ashamed.

It sucked, all this back and forth, all this obsession over my mental health, never quite finding the answers I was looking for.

So, finally, a few months after my un-diagnosis, I decided to seek out a professional assessment.

On the day of my assessment, I tried my best not to mask too much. I let myself rock back and forth, I didn't always make eye contact, I wore comfy clothes and a stimmy necklace, and I answered her questions as honestly as I could manage.

The assessor was kind and attentive and never once dismissed me or invalidated a single thing I said.

But at one point in our interview, she said, "Have you ever thought that you might have ADHD?"

To which I replied, "I mean, sure, but didn't we all think we might have ADHD at the start of the pandemic?"

"No, um, not everyone thought that," she said.

So, moving forward, my autism assessment became an autism and ADHD assessment. We talked, then afterwards she had me and my husband take some tests, and a few weeks later, we met on Zoom, and she diagnosed me not only as autistic but also as ADHD combined type.

It was official. It was in writing. I wasn't just dramatic and sensitive and being silly and obsessive. There it was, on paper, that I was different and had an inherently different experience of this world in pretty much every way.

I wasn't an alien. I wasn't wrong.

I was AuDHD.

Self-diagnosis, professional assessment, and AuDHD identity

Before we enter the discussion on self-diagnosis and professional assessment, which remains a highly contentious topic within the autistic, ADHD, and broader neurodivergent communities, I want to make one thing crystal clear: this book prioritizes self-determination above all else.

How you choose to identify matters so much more than whatever I or any other AuDHDer thinks about how you "should" identify. Every AuDHD person (and every person in general) has the right to say who they are and have others trust that they know themselves better than other people ever could.

That said, I have formed my own opinions on self-diagnosis and professional assessment based on research and on my own and others' lived experience. I'm hopeful that these opinions can be helpful, but if they aren't, please remember: you get to choose who you are. No one, especially not me, can tell you who to be or how to identify.

Self-diagnosis is essential, valid, and more

I wholeheartedly believe in the power of self-diagnosis. Yes, I have a professional diagnosis, but it took me years of trying and being invalidated to get one, not to mention time to research assessors who wouldn't dismiss me again. And, of course, it wasn't free either.

Not everyone has that kind of time, money, or access to affirming clinicians.

Before we can even talk about self-diagnosis being valid, we need to talk about how essential it is.

Professional assessment, especially for autism and for adults, is often pricey. Insurance doesn't always cover adult assessments, resulting in out-of-pocket costs ranging anywhere from $650 to $5000,[3] with the average falling somewhere around $2000.

This expense is compounded by the amount of time necessary to actually do the assessment. Most assessors are only available during a typical workday, meaning you will likely need to take time off of work in order to get assessed, and while some assessments are around 90 minutes, others can last hours, or even be spread out over multiple days.

Many people can't afford the price of assessment, let alone the money lost by taking time off work, and no one should be denied access to their identity because of their economic status. Self-diagnosis is often the only type of diagnosis available to working-class and impoverished people.

But finances and time aren't the only barriers. Even those of us who can afford an assessment may not have access to one in a timely manner. Research shows that, depending on where you live, the waitlist to be assessed for ADHD or autism could range from ten weeks to five years.[4]

Yes, you read that right. Five years. During all that time, what are we supposed to do? Pretend not to know what we know about ourselves? Ignore our needs and refuse to accommodate ourselves? Never speak about our brain or how it works with any confidence?

Finally, even if you manage to get on a short waitlist and you have the cash, you may have a hard time finding an assessor who truly understands autism, ADHD, and AuDHD.

The truth is, even the best doctors are operating with limited information. Much of autism and ADHD research has been historically conducted on young, white, able-bodied, middle-class, cis boys.

If you fall outside of that identity in any way, whether you're an adult or trans or a person of the global majority, then even the best, most well-meaning assessor in the world has limited information to use when diagnosing you.

Not to mention that many of us living in rural areas often have less access to local specialized care, which means we need to travel for our assessment (adding to time and money burdens).

When people try to say self-diagnosis isn't valid, I think they're often overlooking the necessity of it. Poverty, medical racism, or simply living in a rural area are not good reasons people shouldn't be able to claim and talk about their own identity.

However, even if self-diagnosis wasn't the only reasonable option for many of us, it would still be a perfectly valid option.

There is a pervasive belief in much of the world that doctors are objective. This is a huge reason so many people believe self-diagnosis isn't valid—because individuals are unable to be objective about themselves in the way that doctors are.

However, I'm going to argue that while doctors do offer an outside perspective, that perspective is not inherently more objective than your own, nor is it always more accurate. I don't say this to deny the authority, intelligence, or capabilities of doctors. Only to acknowledge their limitations as evidenced by the research.

According to the University of Washington Autism Center, "In our experience...many professionals are not informed about the variety of ways that autism can appear, and often doubt an autistic person's accurate self-identification. In contrast, inaccurate self-identification of autism appears to be uncommon."[5]

Doctors are human, with their own biases that, just like the rest of us, they are often unaware of.

Not to mention the fact that not every doctor, psychologist, or psychiatrist specializes in autism and/or ADHD.

There's no shortage of mental illnesses and mental health struggles out there, and it's impossible for every doctor to specialize in everything. A psychologist who specializes in mood disorders, for example, may not know exactly what to look for when assessing for ADHD beyond the DSM criteria, which we've already established as helpful but limited.

This isn't a failing of the doctor. However, it is their job to say, "I don't know enough to accurately diagnose this; let me put you in contact with someone who does." And in my experience at least, very few doctors actually do this.

I've had several psychiatrists dismiss me over the years, only for me to find out I was absolutely right, and they simply didn't know enough about autism and ADHD to be having any kind of discussion about it with me, let alone telling me definitively that I wasn't AuDHD.

Again, I'm not trying to be a jerk about doctors. Heaven knows when I'm dealing with an illness, I go to the doctor in a heartbeat.

But autism and ADHD aren't illnesses. They're disabilities, identities, neurodivergencies. And they do not require a professional diagnosis in order to be real, and be self-identified.

If you're self-diagnosed, that absolutely "counts" and is real.

So...why get a professional assessment?

With all of this in mind, you might be wondering, "Okay... then why bother getting a professional diagnosis at all?" And that's a great question that all AuDHDers should ask.

Because for some of us, there really isn't a reason. Self-diagnosis does not have to be the first step toward professional diagnosis. It's enough on its own.

However, for many others of us, there are plenty of good reasons to get a professional assessment, so let's talk about it.

First, some AuDHDers need a professional diagnosis in order to receive necessary accommodations and benefits. While some employers and schools will accommodate AuDHDers without official paperwork, many others will not. Plus, as we will discuss in the upcoming chapter on AuDHD and work, AuDHDers are more likely than neurotypical people to be unemployed or underemployed and need government assistance in order to live. In most cases, if not all, you need professional documentation to receive disability benefits.

Second, if you're like me, you need a professional assessment because you've been so thoroughly misdiagnosed, gaslighted, and invalidated about your mental health your whole life that you no longer have enough self-trust to effectively self-diagnose. Are doctors perfect paragons of objectivity? No, not at all. But can the right one be a helpful guide? Yes, absolutely.

And finally, many AuDHDers didn't have a choice in the matter because they were diagnosed in childhood. Unlike today, back in the 80s and 90s, there wasn't much information on autism and ADHD, let alone the kind of support and understanding we have these days.

For instance, did you know that, until 2014, you couldn't be diagnosed as AuDHD?[6] It was believed you could only have autism or ADHD, not both, so if you were diagnosed in childhood and you're over ten years old, there's a very good chance you didn't realize you were AuDHD until you heard about it on social media.

The truth is that our community has been far ahead of the medical community on the common co-occurrence of autism and

ADHD. And now we're getting our chance to share our experiences online, together.

While many early diagnosed AuDHDers were ostracized, bullied, and othered by their peers and parents alike, and, as a result, have come to resent the labels, others have embraced them despite everyone else's rejection, and have become leaders in the neurodiversity movement as it exists today. These leaders may not have a formal AuDHD diagnosis, because when they were diagnosed, that wasn't even allowed. And yet, they are here, leading us, because they have the lived experience necessary to make the change we need to see in the world of neurodivergence and neurodiversity.

Regardless of when or how someone has been diagnosed, it's essential to listen to all kinds of voices in the AuDHD community. Often, late-diagnosed, low support needs AuDHDers are so relieved to have found out who we are and why we're like this that we can sometimes speak over people who have had different experiences, especially those with high support needs, people of the global majority, and early diagnosed AuDHDers.

No matter what kind of AuDHD experience you've had, it's valid. It matters. You matter.

The professional assessment process

Okay, so you've weighed the pros and cons, and decided that professional assessment is the right path for you. Can it really be a positive experience? How can you explain your experience in a way that will make sense to your assessor? What do you do if they say you're not autistic or ADHD?

My assessment was amazing. To this day, my assessor is one of the most competent mental health professionals I've ever worked with, and it's my hope that your assessment can be just as positive.

So, let's talk about how to go about getting a professional assessment done in the most affirming, helpful way possible.

Finding the right assessor

Note: This section is relatively US-centric; however, the basic principles should be applicable worldwide in at least some capacity.

In my experience, many providers will automatically diagnose you with depression and anxiety if your complaints are too vague, but if you're too specific, they'll accuse you of consulting "Dr. Google" and you end up dismissed then too.

These are not the assessors you want to work with if you can help it. You want to be able to have a real, valuable, in-depth conversation about yourself and your brain, right?

Personally, I talked to various therapists and doctors, testing the waters, and abandoning ship if they got spooked by how much I knew about autism, ADHD, and myself. Finally, I found my assessor through the NeuroClastic Directory of Diagnosticians,* and before we even met, I emailed her, telling her I was self-diagnosed, and was she okay with that, and if my assessment results found that I wasn't AuDHD, was she confident she could provide me with a better alternative explanation?

She replied saying that self-diagnosis made total sense to her, and she would help me find my answers, whatever they may be.

That was good enough for me, so I went into the assessment. I highly recommend doing something similar if you're looking to be professionally assessed. Check out the NeuroClastic Directory of Diagnosticians—it's a great global directory, and it even comes with little notes from folks who've been assessed, saying what that particular provider was like. And feel free to email them

---

*   www.neuroclastic.com/diagnosticians

ahead of time with your concerns. Why pay for an initial intake with someone who's going to be unhelpful, or even harmful?

Basically, remember that you're allowed to take up space. You're allowed to be inconvenient. You're allowed to ask for what you need and expect to receive it. In most cases, you're paying a pretty penny for this assessment. Go into it with as good a chance as possible that you'll be heard and understood by selecting an assessor who's willing to really listen to you.

What to say at your assessment

Do you ever have that experience where, in your head, you know exactly what you're struggling with and why, but once someone asks, "What's wrong?" your brain goes completely blank and you're left gesturing vaguely and saying, "I don't know... everything."

That's the last thing you want to happen at your assessment. Which is why I recommend coming prepared. I created an entire binder collecting my self-assessments, the traits I'd noticed and their frequency, how I'd been masking over the years, and so much more. And I brought that bad boy to my assessment.

Now, if I hadn't done my research and found a good assessor, I may have been accused of "shopping" for a diagnosis, or called a hypochondriac, but I did find a good assessor, who took one look at my binder and said, "Man, I wish everyone brought me one of these."

We used the binder to guide our whole interview. She asked about my scores on some of the assessments, some of the questions I highlighted, and, of course, she asked about the traits I'd tracked and how I masked.

It was unbelievably helpful, and I recommend creating your own binder and bringing it with you to your assessment.

(P.S. Not sure where to start on how to make one? I have a

whole YouTube video on how I made mine! Visit www.youtube.com/watch?v=PRnowJH4F3k or scan the QR code.

Reading the results

Getting your assessment results is nerve-wracking. And even if the results are exactly what you expected, it can come with a lot of different emotions.

I know for me, when I read over my diagnostic paperwork the first time, I felt...naked. This person saw more of me than I had ever intentionally showed anyone in my life, and I felt very exposed. It was good to be seen, but I was so used to masking that it did feel a bit weird, and even intrusive.

I recommend taking the day off when you get your results, if you can. Just to process the information, and to cope if the results aren't what you expect.

Many AuDHDers are first diagnosed with one or the other rather than both, so if that is the case for you, don't despair. It's possible that your autism is so strong that it's masking the ADHD, or vice versa, and as you learn to cope with and accommodate yourself, the other will make itself apparent in time. If you feel your results are inaccurate, you can always reach back out to the assessor and present your argument for what you think they missed. They may be willing to reconsider, but they may not.

Remember that self-diagnosis is valid and real, and if you are sure they've missed something and that you truly are AuDHD, you're allowed to live that reality, regardless of your assessment results.

That being said, it's also okay if you find out that you're not AuDHD, but are instead solely autistic or solely ADHD. Even if that feels weird after thinking of yourself as AuDHD for so long, it's okay. The more we know about ourselves, the better, even if it's uncomfortable at first.

What comes after diagnosis??

So, you're AuDHD...now what?

Seriously, what the heck are we supposed to do with this life-changing information? How is it possible that we can receive this paperwork at 2pm and then...what, just turn over laundry and cook dinner like it's a normal day?

Well, if you're like me, it's not.

I literally got my diagnoses, then I went to the store, bought a cookie cake, and asked the person behind the counter to write on it: "Congrats on the autism and ADHD."

She looked confused, but thankfully didn't ask questions.

Then my husband and kiddo and I went out to dinner. It was a day of celebration, because it marked the end of a horrible decade devoured by my obsession with my mental health. Finally, I knew who I was.

But there was also some grief mixed into that celebration. How could my life have been different if I'd known sooner? How was I supposed to make peace with the fact that there was no "getting better" from this? How could I know what was "me" and what was the AuDHD?

And finally, I was a bit lost. I had spent so long searching for answers that it had become my life's mission. With that mission fulfilled, what was I supposed to do next?

So, let's talk about celebration, grief, and confusion around your AuDHD diagnoses.

Diagnosis is worth celebrating

There is so much to celebrate when you finally realize you're AuDHD.

There's the validation of finally understanding *why*. Why everything has been so hard, why nothing has made sense, why people have called you rude or "too loud" or dramatic, when you didn't think you were being any of those things.

There's the validation of seeing yourself as an intentional part of something bigger, rather than an unintentional mistake, isolated and alone.

There's the validation of knowing, for certain, that you're not this way because you're bad at being a person—you are just bad at being a neurotypical person. And that's *okay*.

So celebrate. Celebrate yourself and your brain and your place in this world—not an aberration, but a gift to the universe.

Diagnosis is worth grieving

If that section above didn't sit quite right with you, if it felt wrong, or maybe just...incomplete, then this section should help.

Because it's also okay to grieve your diagnoses.

"But, Megan," you protest, "you just called me a gift to the universe! How could I also grieve this, when it's such a gift??"

It can be both.

You *are* a gift to the universe. And at the same time, AuDHD isn't an easy diagnosis to live with. There are many challenges, from intense sensory aversions and constantly feeling "stuck," to painful boredom and never-ending executive dysfunction. And unlike some other neurodivergent experiences, AuDHD can't be treated or "go into remission." It's forever, all the time.

You can't turn off your autism, not even for a moment, and you will never not be ADHD.

And that's a lot.

It's okay to be sad that you're not "normal."

It's okay to be angry that everyday things are so much harder for you than they are for others.

It's okay to feel like your diagnoses took something away from you. Like knowing about this, as freeing as it is, is also a curse. Because now you can't stop seeing it everywhere, in every part of your life, and who even are you anymore?

This is grief. This is loss. This is AuDHD.

Diagnosis is confusing

You will likely spend the weeks, months, and, honestly, years after your diagnosis (self or professional) recategorizing all your memories into boxes like "Oh shit, that was my autism!" or "Literally, how did nobody notice I was ADHD??"

Eventually, you will likely reach a point where you have no idea where you end and the AuDHD begins.

For many AuDHDers, me included, we start to make peace with that. Personally, I feel that my AuDHD is integral to who I am, and there is no version of me that could ever exist without AuDHD. I would be such a different person that I would no longer be "me."

However, many other AuDHDers do feel that their autism and ADHD are separate entities from their sense of self, and may spend significant time and energy sorting out what feels like "me" vs. what feels like something "other."

No matter which way you feel, it's okay. You don't have to feel any particular way about your diagnosis. It's okay to be happy and sad and confused at the same time.

But you don't have to just sit in your feelings forever. There are practical things you can do to help you better understand and embrace your diagnosis, if you like.

Practical action #1: Find your people

There are so many incredible creators out there speaking their AuDHD truth, and listening to their truths is one of the key ways I was able to find mine.

Learning from others' lived experiences can be absolutely life-changing, because while research is valuable, it's often slow to catch up and draws an incomplete picture of autism and ADHD.

Namely, people of the global majority, multiply disabled folks, adults, trans and gender-nonconforming folks, and so many other groups of people are routinely (and intentionally) left out of the research.

So, how many conclusions can we really draw from the research anyway? Is it fair to ask a 63-year-old trans woman from Ghana to extrapolate information gleaned from studying eight-year-old cis boys from Michigan? How much of that information will really apply to her?

Research is wonderful—I'm a major research nerd (as evidenced by the extensive source list of this book) *and* I also recognize that if we only learn about neurodivergence from the research, we are only getting part of the picture.

And that's where lived experience and learning from other people comes in.

Find your people online—people who look and act like you and can reflect your experience back to you.

You can do this by searching social media or search engines for "AuDHD" and something about yourself, like "AuDHD 30-something woman," "AuDHD and gender-nonconforming" or "AuDHD hand-eye coordination issues." Find creators who speak to you and your experience, and enjoy seeing yourself finally being mirrored and understood.

There are also communities out there you can join, like Facebook groups, Discord servers, and more. Again, a quick search in your favorite search engine should turn up several of these groups, many of which are specific to particular genders, cultures, or occupations.

Next, make sure you're also finding your people who look different from you, live in different places than you, and have experiences that differ from your own. These are your people too. Even if you have less in common than you share, you share something pretty major: autism and/or ADHD.

Personally, I've gained a much more nuanced understanding of so many things because of the variety of voices I follow and listen to. For example, take ABA (applied behavioral analysis, a widely studied and widely debated form of therapy for autism): I've listened to autistic people who've been through it and consider it a form of abuse, to autistic people who didn't go through ABA but wish they had, to Black families who see ABA as one of the only ways to help keep their autistic family members safe, and Black autistic people who roundly reject ABA, and so many others.

I've also gained a ton of perspective on the double-empathy problem.[7] In short, researchers studied the way autistic folks communicate with other autistic folks, and how allistic (non-autistic) folks communicate with other allistic folks, and then looked at how autistic and allistic folks communicate with each other.

The study found that communication was equally effective in the all-autistic and all-allistic groups, and communication only really broke down in the autistic-allistic mixed group.

Many white, low support needs autistic folks point to this and say, "See! We don't have communication deficits, we just communicate differently!" But nonspeaking, non-white, and/or high support needs autistic folks—none of whom were included in the double-empathy problem study by the way—often have a very different perspective on it. Namely, that many autistic folks do have communication deficits, and we shouldn't be focusing on what's a deficit and what's a difference, but rather accepting autistic people as whole people, regardless of their abilities.

What I'm trying to say is, seek out people who are different from you and listen to them. Not only do their stories matter inherently, but also they will give you a much more complete and nuanced understanding of AuDHD.

Practical action #2: Work with a neuro-affirming professional

Books, journaling, and driving around scream-singing to that one song that's always made us feel a little too seen are all great ways to get to know ourselves and heal some of the trauma many of us have from growing up AuDHD.

But it's also okay to get some help from a professional.

There are all kinds of helpers out there. In this section, we'll primarily focus on therapists and coaches, but there are other helping professions that could be beneficial for you too, like:

- occupational therapy
- reiki
- massage therapy
- psychiatry
- hypnosis
- speech therapy.

I'm sure there are many more helping professions I'm missing, but hopefully this list is a good start.

Personally, the majority of my healing work has taken place in therapy or with coaches. I'm a life coach myself, and I have a lot of advice on how to pick the right therapist or coach for you, and how to get the most out of your time with them.

If you're interested in finding a neuro-affirming therapist or coach, check out Resources for AuDHDers at the end of this book.

In the meantime, here are some of the best "green flags" I've noticed in coaches and therapists—AKA signs that they are actually neuro-affirming.

Green flag #1: Transparency, especially around their scope of practice

If a therapist or coach tells you which areas they specialize in, and which areas they are less equipped to handle, knowing full well they might lose your business if you happen to struggle in one of the areas where they just admitted they're less qualified, that's a good helper.

No therapist or coach, no matter how educated or experienced, can specialize in everything. Nothing sets off my red-flag siren like seeing a therapist listed on Psychology Today who has listed literally everything under "Specializations."

Honesty is just super important when working with a helper, because you need to be able to trust them if you're going to open up to them. And if they are more dedicated to making sure you get the help you need, even if it's not with them, rather than being dedicated to getting another client on their roster, that's always a green flag for me.

Green flag #2: Uses up-to-date neurodivergent symbols and language

This one isn't a deal-breaker for me if I don't see it, but it always makes me feel better when I do. The AuDHD world is always evolving, and while I know it can be a pain for providers to constantly update their website to reflect changes in symbolism or language to reflect that evolution, it really indicates to me that this person knows their stuff and is in touch with the community.

For example, if I saw a website prominently featuring the infinity sign (the modern symbol for neurodivergence), talking about support needs, and *not* mentioning things like "ADD" or functioning labels (which are generally out-of-date terms that the neurodivergent community no longer widely uses), that would tell me that this provider, regardless of when they received their training initially, has continued educating themselves.

I know I won't spend half my appointment explaining current nomenclature to them, and I might actually learn from them instead.

Green flag #3: They use inclusive and accepting language for all kinds of neurodivergence, even ones I don't experience

I expect my provider to support all kinds of neurodivergent people, not just me, and not just AuDHDers. For example, I feel I can learn a lot from how a provider speaks about borderline personality disorder, a condition I used to think I had before I learned I was AuDHD.

A green flag might look like the provider focusing on what BPD feels like for the person who has it, and validating the emotional pain that often accompanies BPD, and maybe even talking about how the entire concept of a personality being disordered may be an unhelpful framework for understanding people who have likely been through extensive trauma.

On the other hand, if a provider said BPD was "untreatable," which is an objectively untrue statement that many therapists use as an excuse not to treat their BPD clients with respect and dignity, then I would not consider that inclusive language for all kinds of neurodivergence.

Personally, I don't want a therapist or coach who is only understanding of my particular neurodivergence while holding stigmatizing beliefs about other types of neurodivergence. We rise together or not at all.

Working with a therapist or coach: My favorite tips

I've been in therapy for over a decade. Plus, I've had a coach for the last four years too. So I'm not just telling you what I like my coaching clients to do; I'm telling you what I've had to do to get the most out of my own therapy and coaching. Here are my top three tips:

- **Remember that this is about you.** Your therapist or coach consented to this situation and is being fairly compensated for their efforts, so don't waste your time worrying about whether you're selfish or needy or "too much." In fact, if you can't shake those fears, bring this up with your coach or therapist. They can likely help you work through it so that you get more out of your time with them.

- **Practice rupture and repair.** This is something I avoided for so long, but since I've started practicing this, I've improved my relationships not only with my therapists and coaches but also with other people in my life. The idea of rupture and repair is that all relationships have moments of rupture, where the relationship is damaged and the people involved experience emotional distance from each other. This is wholly unavoidable, and it happens even in the healthiest of relationships because no two people are exactly alike and are bound to disagree, and no one is flawless and will never mess up in their relationships.

  Enter, repair. The most helpful way to respond when rupture happens is for both people to dedicate themselves to bridging the gap through repair—talking about your feelings, of course, but also talking about what led to the rupture, like old patterns both of you might be playing out in the relationship. The thing is, in real life, doing this is hard. Like, really hard. So, a great place to practice it is in therapy or coaching. Your therapist or coach is going to mess up at some point, say or do something hurtful, and you're going to feel tempted to either stop working with them or pretend it didn't bother you. I encourage you to try repair instead (assuming they didn't intentionally do harm or cross a line you aren't interested in repairing, of course). Tell them how what they said made you feel, tell them you're scared to be honest about this, tell them why it's so upsetting for you. Just word vomit, honestly. Let them worry about making it all make sense.

- **Do the work between sessions.** I'll be honest: I struggle with this one. I'm just not great with follow-through (as I'm sure you understand, if you're reading this). But I get the most out of coaching or therapy when I do the in-between work. The journaling, the reflection, the stuff you do when you're not in crisis, but rather trying to prevent yourself from getting to that point. One common experience for folks with ADHD is something colloquially called "emotional object permanence." You know how babies don't always realize something exists when it's not in their line of sight? Yeah, a lot of ADHDers experience that with our emotions. If we aren't currently in crisis, we can't really imagine being in that headspace. So we don't always see the point of doing the work in between coaching or therapy sessions. But I'm working on journaling a few times a week now, and I can honestly say it makes a tremendous difference to reflect on things, even when I'm okay. It gives me so much more to bring to my sessions so that I get more out of the experience.

EXERCISES

→ List ten things about your AuDHD that make you "you" (e.g. "I'm scatterbrained because of ADHD, which often makes me creative" or "My autism makes me very particular, which makes me great at dealing with details").

- Alternatively, if you feel like your AuDHD is separate from you, write ten things that are definitively "you" and *not* your AuDHD (e.g. "I am creative, and would be regardless of whether I was autistic or ADHD" or "My kindness has nothing to do with my diagnoses").

→ Create an art piece that describes your feelings about the diagnosis. Feel free to create something literal, like a self-portrait showing how your face expresses your feelings about the diagnosis, or something more abstract (I highly recommend finger painting if you're a sensory-seeking kind of person!).

→ Write an obituary for your "neurotypical" self who never truly existed.

KEY TAKEAWAYS

→ Diagnosis is rarely a straightforward path.

→ Self-diagnosis is valid, and so is professional diagnosis. Both paths can be helpful.

→ The NeuroClastic Directory of Diagnosticians is a global directory that can help you find an assessor.

→ Celebration, grief, and confusion are all valid responses to diagnosis.

→ It's vital to learn from other AuDHDers who are like and unlike you.

There are so many different types of helpers out there who can help you as an AuDHDer. You're not alone in this.

Part 2
Living with AuDHD

CHAPTER 3

Day-to-Day Life with AuDHD

The amazing and unbelievable thing about diagnosis is that regular, day-to-day life just…goes on afterwards. If you've ever lost a loved one or gotten engaged or graduated school, you know how it is. The big thing happens, and you expect everything to be different afterwards, and in some ways it is, but in a lot of ways, life just continues.

And this chapter will be all about what that life looks like. Because even if you just recently found out the name for it, you've always been AuDHD, and your daily life is going to look a little different from that of a neurotypical.

There are five key aspects of daily life that I want to be sure we touch on in this chapter, and they are:

1. housework
2. self-care
3. social life
4. hobbies
5. parenting.

Each of these categories is going to look completely different for you, an AuDHDer, than it does for a neurotypical. If you've been trying to hold yourself to neurotypical standards in all of these categories, and you've been feeling like a failure, I want to offer you a metaphor.

Pretend all the neurotypical folks in the world are playing baseball. Baseball has rules, and generally speaking, our society expects everyone to play by those rules.

But you're not neurotypical. Your brain and body were hard-wired to play tennis. Tennis has *very* different rules from baseball. If you tried to play tennis using baseball rules, or if you tried to play baseball using tennis equipment, you'd definitely fail.

But that's not because you're bad at either sport. It's because you've set unhelpful expectations not based on the reality of your situation.

In plain language, here's what I mean: you're not failing at being an adult. You're not failing at all. You're just not neurotypical. And accepting that you're neurodivergent doesn't mean you're "lowering expectations" or something; it just means you're being honest about the tools you do and don't have, and the rules you do and don't understand.

Accepting that you're different doesn't mean admitting that you're less-than. Accepting your differences is actually the only way to live your own life, instead of the one others expect you to live.

Housework

Cleaning is the worst.

I do not do it as often as I should, or even as often as I want to, largely because of my AuDHD. It's a sensory nightmare, it requires a level of executive functioning that I very rarely possess, and if you live with other people, there's a social element that can lead to frustration or even resentment.

From microfiber cloths to strong chemical odors, cleaning is not a pleasant sensory experience for most AuDHDers. Personally, my least favorite sensory experience when it comes to cleaning?

The sensation of having just dried my hands, so they're still just a tiny bit wet, and then touching dry paper towels. Hell on Earth, let me tell you.

Many autistic folks are hypersensitive to all kinds of sensory experiences, and many ADHDers can't sift through which input is important, so we pay attention to all of it. Take these traits together, and it means that many AuDHDers can't help but pay attention to sensory sensations that many neurotypical people simply ignore, or don't even notice in the first place.

In order to clean our space, AuDHDers must willingly submit ourselves to sensations that will cause us irritation, overwhelm, and even distress.

While much of the sensory experience of cleaning is unavoidable, there are several things we can do as AuDHDers to cope. Some folks can use gloves while cleaning in order to avoid unpleasant textures, though many of us, myself included, find gloves to be an unpleasant texture in and of themselves, so that may be a non-starter.

An alternative that's helped me has been an electric scrubbing wand. This keeps me from having to touch horrible microfiber towels, plus it keeps my hands mostly dry, which is preferable for me. However, this means I have to remember to charge it before I need to clean, which, let's be honest, rarely happens thanks to ADHD.

This is a prime example of the unique overlap between autistic and ADHD traits that just isn't often addressed when folks talk about only autism or only ADHD. A solution that may help with the sensory issues, like an electric scrubbing wand, may be difficult or impossible to keep up with due to ADHD issues with executive functioning, like having to remember to charge it.

And, of course, there's the social element of cleaning. The

truth is, many AuDHDers had negative experiences with cleaning when we were growing up, and we bring those experiences with us into our adult relationships as well.

For example, when you were little, did your parents tell you to "clean your room," with no further instruction or details? And did you stare blankly at your room, which looked like a tornado had gone through it, totally at a loss to know where to start or what to do?

This is a very common AuDHD experience.

The autistic side of our brain needs detailed instructions because we don't naturally fill in the blanks. "Clean your room" is so vague as to be basically meaningless to us. And the ADHD side of our brain needs some kind of funnel for our attention so that we don't get overwhelmed by the chaotic amount of stimulation provided by all the mess.

But many of us didn't know why "clean your room" wasn't a helpful instruction, so we couldn't ask for more details, or if we did try to ask for help, we were further chided. Our parents might have been frustrated we couldn't do something we "should" have been able to do at that age, or maybe they thought we were just trying to get them to do it for us. When really, we just truly needed help.

As a result, we would try and usually fail to clean our room (and heaven help you if you were raised with someone with strict, but never explicitly stated, cleanliness standards). And that failure combined with the confusion and overwhelm led to an increased disdain for cleaning that many of us have carried into adulthood.

Partners, caregivers, or roommates may expect us to know how to clean, since we're adults, when, in reality, we never learned how to clean in a way that actually works for us. We've always just failed at it, and probably learned to avoid it as well.

This can lead to arguments with the people we live with, as they may feel an unfair amount of the cleaning burden is falling to them.

And the thing is, they may not be wrong.

Even though we have very good reasons for avoiding cleaning, from sensory aversions to executive dysfunction to childhood wounds, it's still unfair to expect others to clean up after us without having an explicit conversation about that expectation.

For some AuDHDers, myself included, there are certain elements of cleaning we simply cannot do. For example, I can't do laundry. I let it pile up until there are upwards of ten loads that need to be done, so I try to get them done as quickly as possible and dump the clothes in the washer without checking them. I've ruined many pairs of wireless headphones, and on more than one occasion, I've washed underwear with poop in them from a kiddo potty-training mishap.

I keep thinking I'll get better at it, that each time it's just a fluke, a one-time thing, but then it happens again and again and again. So, finally, my husband and I talked about it, and he took over responsibility for the laundry.

It's okay if there are things you can't do. It's alright to admit defeat, to stop smashing your head up against a brick wall, and let others help you. But you have to talk to them about it.

Before my husband and I talked about the laundry situation, things would usually go like this:

Husband: *makes vague mention of laundry needing to be done*

Me: *grumbles something about doing it soon, knowing full well I won't do it until I'm out of underwear*

Me: *does laundry, poorly, things get ruined*

Husband: *is frustrated, but trying not to show it because he could have done the laundry and didn't, so doesn't feel like he has a right to complain about how I do it*

Me: *picks up on that unstated frustration and gets frustrated back, but also tries not to show it because he didn't say anything, so what am I even mad about?*

And it would repeat every few weeks.

It was super great for our marriage, as you can probably guess.

Now that we've gotten all our frustrations out in the open and found a solution that works better for us (AKA him doing the laundry to begin with), things are much, much better. In exchange, I've taken over cleaning bathrooms, a chore that he was previously in charge of.

Is it my favorite? No, not at all. But I am far more capable of cleaning the bathroom well than I am of doing laundry well. So that's what works for us.

When it comes to the social pitfalls of cleaning, my biggest piece of advice is to be explicit about your needs and expectations, and ask others to do the same. The worst arguments I've ever been in were almost always the result of miscommunications or built-up resentment from unspoken expectations.

Self-care

Right off the bat, I'm going to separate self-care into two main categories: practical self-care and luxurious self-care.

Self-care can totally look like bubble baths and smutty books and buying shit you don't need from the Target dollar spot. But it also looks like eating a vegetable every now and again, changing your sheets, and getting some sleep.

Neither one of these forms of self-care is necessarily better than the other, and we need them both, but to get the most out of our self-care, we need to know what our goal is: to take care of ourselves in a practical way, or to treat ourselves extra nice and gentle.

When it comes to practical self-care, there are a few strategies that I think are especially helpful for AuDHDers:

- nervous system regulation
- treating yourself like a houseplant (I'll explain in a minute, promise)
- validation.

Let's start with nervous system regulation, because, honestly, it's hard to do anything at all when your nervous system feels like you're being hunted for sport when you're really just trying to eat a new food.

Many AuDHDers are especially prone to nervous system dysregulation because we live in a high-stimulus world now, with lots of lights, sounds, scents, and textures that can overstimulate us. However, even if we lived in a more low-stimulus world, we would likely be prone to nervous system dysregulation, as our nervous systems are simply more sensitive to input in many cases.[1]

Some of my favorite ways to soothe my nervous system include:

- throwing ice cubes at the bathtub or at my back patio (watching something shatter when you're upset is very cathartic)
- singing Broadway songs at the top of my lungs (singing encourages deep breathing and self-expression, both of which can help you regulate)
- lying flat on my back on the floor (no idea why this works, but it does)
- taking deep breaths, then exhaling as slowly as possible (slow exhales are not possible if you're running away from a predator, so the slow exhale signals to your nervous system that you're safe)

- dancing to music that sounds happy but has sad lyrics (this combination of happy and sad is super regulating for me, though I couldn't explain why)
- using an ice roller on my face, or placing a frozen bag of peas on my chest or the back of my neck (ice helps reduce overstimulation)
- wrapping a heating pad around my stomach (heat helps bring your nervous system back online if you're feeling dissociated or numb)
- taking a hot shower (same thing, with the heat).

Once you've brought your nervous system to a level that feels more manageable, you can try one of my favorite self-care strategies: treating yourself like a houseplant.

If you're a plant parent, think of how you look after your plants. You water them regularly, make sure they get the right amount of sunlight for their unique needs, and repot them as they grow and require more space.

You might grumble about having to do these things, or, since you have ADHD, you might forget sometimes, but generally speaking, you don't make your plant's needs mean anything negative about the plant. It's not needy or stupid or "too much."

It's just a plant. It just needs what it needs.

What if you treated yourself that way?

What if you fed yourself and drank water, not because you wanted to but because you knew you needed it?

What if you took care of your environment—again, not because you want to necessarily, but because you knew you needed it?

When we think of ourselves as a houseplant, we are able to treat our needs as neutral, instead of as some kind of problem. It allows us to see practical self-care as a gentle, understated form of love, rather than just another item on our to-do list.

Many AuDHDers are very sensitive to their environments, much like a houseplant, and when we give ourselves permission to be that way, to be sensitive without judgment, we can take better care of that sensitivity.

Finally, speaking of sensitivity, the last form of practical self-care that AuDHDers need is validation.

Raise your hand if you've ever been called "dramatic," "too sensitive," or "exaggerating."

Yeah, me too. All the time growing up.

This kind of talk is incredibly invalidating because it basically says that our perceptions and experiences are not an accurate reflection of reality as agreed upon by everyone else. We are weird, we are "other," we are wrong. And when you are invalidated over a long period of time, as many AuDHDers are, it can foster a deep distrust of ourselves. And when we don't trust ourselves, we often outsource our version of reality to others.

This looks like people pleasing, masking, imposter syndrome, self-loathing, and so much more. When we don't trust ourselves, we let other people tell us who we are and what we want and what is real. And that is not only deeply invalidating, but it can also be dangerous.

Studies show that autistic folks especially are more likely than allistic people to experience abusive relationships.[2] And one reason for this, among many others, is the lack of self-trust that we foster through years of invalidation. If you've spent your whole life listening to others over your own intuition, how would you ever know for sure whether someone is treating you poorly or if you're just being "dramatic" again?

Validation is not a luxury for AuDHDers—it's a necessity. When we are able to say, "No, I'm not dramatic, I'm perceptive and I process things deeply, and there is nothing wrong with that," we don't just feel better about ourselves, we keep ourselves safer as well.

Unlike practical self-care, which I think is largely the same for all kinds of AuDHDers, luxurious self-care really depends on what you find "luxurious."

For me, it's getting acrylic nails done. I absolutely adore acrylic nails and get them done at least twice a year, more if my nails (and wallet) can handle it.

But I know lots of AuDHDers who absolutely hate acrylic nails because the process of having someone else do their nails feels way too awkward, plus they can't tune out the feeling of the fake nails on their real nails (there's that lack of habituation we talked about in Chapter 1!).

Similarly, I know some AuDHDers who love reading as a form of self-care. They just lose themselves in a book and it brings them so much joy and leaves them feeling totally zen. But for me, reading requires entirely too much focus, and therefore is more of a task than a form of self-care for me most of the time.

So, for luxurious self-care, I recommend coming up with three lists: one for daily luxuries, one for weekly luxuries, and one for monthly or quarterly luxuries.

Need some help thinking of little luxuries? Here are some of my favorites:

Daily:

- Stim singing/dancing/spinning/etc.
- Finger painting
- Junk journaling
- Fancy coffee
- Nature hike
- Cry
- Read
- Watch YouTube
- Listen to a podcast
- Stretch

Weekly:

- Bake cookies
- Walk around the mall, get a pretzel
- Therapy/coaching/engage with a helper of some kind
- Go to the library
- Explore a new local shop
- Watch your favorite movie
- Watch a new movie
- "Everything shower" (AKA do all the luxurious things, like deep conditioning your hair, shaving your legs, maybe even a face mask!)
- Take a bath
- Go to the gym

Monthly/Quarterly:

- Get a massage
- Get your nails done
- Visit a loved one
- Go on a date (with a loved one or on your own! See a movie, go to dinner, hang out at a bookstore—whatever feels right!)
- Book club
- Take a weekend trip to a location less than two hours away and try all the local coffee!
- Bring $10 to a dollar store or thrift store and see if you can find any treasures.

Social life

Can we be honest for a minute? It's really hard to have a social life as an AuDHDer.

Many AuDHDers are introverted (meaning they gain energy from being alone and tend to lose energy by being with people). But even for those of us who are extroverted and gain energy from being around people, like me, social events are fraught with social cues we're bound to miss, sensory experiences that will likely overwhelm us, and executive functioning obstacles that make it near impossible to get there on time.

And yet a social support network is essential for all humans, especially those of us who have always felt othered. We need to feel included and seen and like we can rely on others.

And getting out of the house is part of that. So, let's talk about how to be social while also being gentle with yourself and paying attention to your AuDHD needs.

First, if getting out of the house is a huge obstacle for you, whether it's due to limited transportation options, agoraphobia, physical disability, or something else, then find community online.

Personally, I run a pay-what-you-can monthly membership called The Neurodivergent Clubhouse that's designed to help all kinds of neurodivergent people (including AuDHDers) find like-minded folks that you can talk to, relate to, and get advice from. We do group coaching, a book club, body doubling, and so much more. Visit www.theneurocuriosityclub.com/nd-clubhouse or scan the QR code to learn more. 

Other online communities include the Hiki app,* which helps connect all kinds of neurodivergent people; plus, it allows you to choose whether you're looking for dating, friendship, or community!

I also highly recommend checking out Resources for AuD-HDers at the end of this book to find neurodivergent content

---

* www.hikiapp.com

creators, many of whom offer their own communities where you can meet your fellow neurodivergent people!

But let's say you're trying to use your phone a little less, trying to connect with people IRL (in real life), and wanting to have somewhere to be besides your own home.

How can you get out of the house and navigate the social, sensory, and executive functioning challenges that leaving the house entails?

Social cues

When you're AuDHD, you have all kinds of social struggles. This is often attributed to autism, since autistic folks are more likely to miss social cues, such as someone asking you questions and expecting you to ask them questions in return, compared to our allistic peers.

But ADHD can play into social issues as well. ADHD is associated with impulsivity and inattentiveness, which can lead to frequent interrupting or zoning out during a conversation, which seem rude to others, even though we aren't doing it on purpose.

And when you're AuDHD, you're dealing with both. You simply do not perceive most social cues because of autism, and even when you do perceive social cues, you're often unable to do what's expected because of ADHD.

The thought of having to monitor your behavior and do everything "right" even if it doesn't feel natural is a pretty good deterrent for going out. But I think there are ways to be more comfortable socially while you're out.

First, determine which people you feel most comfortable around, the people who know you well and know that when you interrupt or miss a social cue, you're not being rude—you're just being AuDHD. When you're feeling super low-energy but still want social interaction, these are the people you should call. When you have more energy, you can try hanging out with people you're less close to and might require more effort on your part.

Second, start educating the people you love about your social style. For example, I've told several of my friends that I tend to relate to others through my current hyperfixations and special interests. So, if I'm going on and on about my favorite TV show or social issue, I'm not trying to dominate the conversation with my interests, but I'm trying to use my interests to connect with them.

And finally, check out Chapter 6: To Mask or Not to Mask. Many of us hide our AuDHD traits, and that can make socializing especially exhausting, because we're hiding the whole time. Learning to unmask in ways that feel safe and good can help make socializing more feasible.

Sensory environment

A lot of the time, when people want to go out, especially when you're in your 20s, they want to go to a bar or a club or some other loud, sticky, crowded place.

All of which can be a bit of a nightmare for many AuDHDers. Our autism can make us hypersensitive to many sensory experiences, like loud music, shouted conversations, or strong smells. And our ADHD makes it impossible to sift through all that sensory input and decide which is most important. Instead, it all floods our senses and often overwhelms us.

My first tip for this problem is to simply not go to bars or clubs (unless you're more of a sensory-seeking person who enjoys all that sensory input). But I know sometimes the people we love enjoy that stuff and we want to be there with them. So, how can we make these loud, crowded places more manageable for our AuDHD?

First, invest in a pair of noise-reducing earplugs. You don't want noise canceling necessarily, because you still want to be able to hear the conversations with your own friends, but you want to try to block out the clinking of glasses and bumping bass of the music. Personally, I love my Loop earplugs, but I know others enjoy Flare or Eargasm earplugs as well.

Second, dress comfortably. If tight clothes make you feel safe and contained, then wear those. But on the other hand, if tight clothes make you feel claustrophobic or irritated, then wear nice, loose clothes instead. I used to dress for looks over comfort, and I absolutely had more meltdowns and was more exhausted by the end of the day. Now, I wear whatever feels comfy and appropriately stimulating for me. For instance, right now, I'm wearing a giant, soft jumpsuit and an oversized fluffy sweater, both of which are brightly colored. The colors give me a great dopamine boost, and the soft, oversized nature of everything keeps me from feeling constricted and uncomfortable.

Finally, if you're particularly sensitive to scent, dab a small amount of a pleasant scent under your nose, right above your upper lip, before going out. I know some folks who use a little bit of Vick's VapoRub, but if that's too strong (or if you hate that smell, like me), you can use diluted essential oils or even a scented lip balm to help provide you with a scent you find tolerable to help block out the other scents of going out.

Executive functioning

The last major hurdle many AuDHDers experience when it comes to having a social life is executive dysfunction. This often makes us late to social events, either because we couldn't accurately perceive the passage of time, or because we got caught up in a million side quests when trying to get ready and out the door.

While executive dysfunction is primarily an ADHD struggle, autism can affect it in interesting ways. For example, the ADHD part of my brain might be struggling to figure out what I need to do before I leave for a social outing, but my autism will often compound this struggle by trying to tell me there's a "correct" way to do all the things I have to do before I leave.

I call this "step thinking." Autism likes to tell us that there are specific steps we must take, and that we must take them in a specific order.

This makes executive dysfunction that much harder, because while one part of your brain is trying to figure out *what* needs to be done, the other half of your brain is trying to tell you exactly *how* to do it all. It's a lot like trying to do a puzzle without a picture to reference, plus you're missing half the pieces.

So, how can we cope with all this and actually get to our social obligations on time (or at least fashionably late instead of annoyingly late or so late we miss them entirely)?

Don't worry, you won't hear me telling you to set another alarm or reminder. Odds are, you're already doing that. You need some more creative solutions.

First, keep your "going out" routine written down or typed in an easily accessible place. There are all kinds of routine apps you can use to keep track of all the steps it takes to go out, or you can write it down on a piece of paper and tape it to your mirror.

Having trouble getting started? Here's what my going out routine looks like:

- Decide if I need to shower
  - When did I shower last?
  - Do I feel clean?
  - Is it okay if my hair is wet where I'm going?
  - Do I have energy to both shower and go out?
- Shower if needed
- Makeup and hair
  - Low energy: leave hair wet, no makeup
  - Medium energy: leave hair wet, minimal makeup

- - High energy: dry and style hair, full face of makeup
- Pick out clothes (see sensory section! dress comfortably!)
- Pack bag
  - Wallet
  - Keys
  - Phone
  - Phone charger
  - Protein bar
  - Anything needed for where I'm going
- Leave time to get gas, odds are good that your fuel light is on!

I also highly recommend creating a schedule, working backwards from the time you need to be somewhere.

For example, if I need to be at a bar for a poetry slam by 8pm, then the first thing I consider is how long it takes to drive there. If it takes 20 minutes, then I know I have to leave by 7:40pm. Then I look at my going-out routine. I can estimate that it will take me a minimum of 30 minutes to do all of that, which means I need to start getting ready by 7:10pm. Then I like to throw in a ten-minute buffer, just in case. So, if I want to be at the bar by 8pm, I need to start getting ready at 7pm.

Now, you might be tempted to just get ready at 6pm—that way you have plenty of extra buffer time, but in my experience, this is a mistake. If you start getting ready at 6pm, you have a full extra hour. Even if you take your time, you'll likely have at least 20 minutes of downtime before you have to leave.

This is the danger zone. This is where we sit down and turn on YouTube "just for a second." And next thing we know, it's 8:30pm and we've missed our time slot for the poetry slam.

It's tricky. You don't want to give yourself so little time that you can't actually get everything done, but you don't want to give yourself too much time so that you end up losing track of time.

Personally, if I'm feeling really low-energy, or if my executive dysfunction has been particularly bad, then I'll give myself a 30-minute buffer instead of ten minutes. But I never give myself less than a ten-minute buffer. With AuDHD, something is going to come up and eat up those minutes, I am pretty much certain.

Hobbies

Our lives are so much more than just school and work, and because autism and ADHD affect every aspect of life, it makes sense that they would affect all those things we do outside of school and work too.

So many frustrated parents, spouses, and teachers only see our struggles in the classroom or with housework. They don't see the 2am meltdowns when we're exhausted and know we need to turn our game off and get some sleep, but we just can't. They don't see how we stare at the same paragraph in our book for over an hour, trying to get our brain to make sense of the words. They don't see how we struggle to do the things we enjoy too, not just the "boring" stuff.

Why are hobbies so hard for AuDHDers? As with every other section in this chapter, it's because of the unique way our autism and ADHD interact with each other. ADHD generally makes starting pretty much any task harder due to executive dysfunction. But ADHD presents another struggle: the effects of repeated "failure."

Jessica McCabe, from the YouTube channel "How to ADHD," calls this the "wall of awful."* Basically, every time we fail to turn in our homework on time or show up for practice on the right day or listen quietly when a friend is talking, a brick gets added to our "wall of awful." This wall stands in our way any time we try

---

* www.youtube.com/@HowtoADHD

to start anything, including our hobbies. It creates a core belief about ourselves that says "I am incompetent."

This core belief stops us from even trying, because we believe it's pointless. We have failed enough times that it feels like our fate is sealed. We are doomed to fail at everything, not because we're catastrophizing or being overly self-critical, but because we have real, actual evidence that we have failed before, and very little evidence saying that we might succeed in future attempts.

Did you know that, on average, ADHD kids receive over 20,000 critical messages before age 12?[3]

That's a lot of criticism. And it might be part of the reason behind something called rejection sensitive dysphoria (RSD). As mentioned in Chapter 1 on updating the ADHD criteria, RSD is not currently an official criterion for diagnosing ADHD, but it is very popular in the ADHD community.

Basically, RSD is increased sensitivity to rejection so that, instead of feeling like a painful sting, it can feel all-consuming and terrible. Rather than thinking, "Oof, I got rejected, that sucked," we often think, "I got rejected because I am a horrible person who deserves to be rejected."

There's a lot of debate on whether RSD is just an inherent part of the ADHD brain, or whether it's the result of increased critical messages received throughout childhood (and beyond). But regardless of why we experience RSD, it's clear that we do, and this can make it harder for us to do all kinds of things, including the things we enjoy.

Finally, we need to address how our autism plays into hobbies as well. Many autistic folks develop special interests that are deep and long-lasting. We can completely lose ourselves in our hobbies for hours, sometimes days at a time.

And this isn't always good for us. We might forget to use the restroom until it becomes an absolute emergency, or forget to eat until we're lightheaded, or forget about our other very important obligations.

As a result, sometimes autistic folks will avoid our hobbies. Even though they bring us so much joy, we're afraid of getting lost in them to the point that we're not being healthy anymore. We aren't sure how to engage in our hobbies lightly, so we avoid them entirely to make sure we eat and sleep and all that.

Overall, AuDHDers can often feel a profound sense of defeat around their hobbies. It's a lose-lose: either we're going to try to do something and fail (ADHD) or we're going to try something and get totally sucked in and fail in other areas of our life (autism).

No matter what we do, we suck.

This isn't true, of course, but that's how it feels a lot of the time. So, what can we do? How can we enjoy our hobbies and have fun without feeling like a failure?

First, practice your hobbies in secret. Tell no one about them; just do them for yourself, by yourself for a while. Not only will this reduce any potential criticism, but it will also provide a nice little dopamine boost, since sneaky secrets are always a bit of a thrill.

Second, try building in "exit ramps" on your hobbies—that way you don't get stuck in hyperfocus to the point that you get dizzy or can't make it to the bathroom in time.

One way I build in exit ramps on digital activities is having unrelated tabs open. If I'm working on writing this book, for example, and I'm afraid I'll get sucked into it for hours, I'll leave my business software open as well. Then there's at least a chance I'll glance down at my task bar, see the business software, and click over there for just a moment. That creates a kind of "exit ramp" so that I can take a break from writing long enough to become aware of my bodily needs or other scheduled obligations.

The same concept applies to non-digital hobbies. Try setting something in your line of sight that will remind you to take breaks.

I like to leave protein bars on my desk while I color, or read in the same room as my partner, and when he goes to the bathroom, I try to go right after.

Finally, create bite-sized ways to engage with your hobbies. Instead of broadly saying "I'm going to read," maybe tell yourself, "I'm going to read five chapters." Or instead of saying "I'm going to crochet," maybe say instead, "I'm going to crochet ten rows."

Will you stick to that? Probably not, but it will act kind of like a rope, keeping you in the vicinity of where you want to be. Even if you end up reading ten chapters, that's probably still better than reading the whole book and staying up until 3am. Even if you crochet 50 rows, that's better than finishing the whole project in one sitting and then collapsing for three days.

You deserve to have a life outside of school and work. You deserve to be able to engage in your hobbies and have fun. Hopefully, these tips will help make it just a bit easier.

Parenting

Finally, if we're going to talk about day-to-day life as an AuDHDer, we have to talk about parenting. If you're not a parent, no worries, feel free to skip this section, but if you are, you know how hard parenting can be when you're both autistic and ADHD. As a mother of three, including one-year-old twins, I am very familiar with the stress of being an AuDHD parent. So, let's talk about some of the most common frustrations among AuDHD parents and what we can do about them.

Overstimulation

Tell me, is this familiar?

It's 6pm. You've got dinner on the stove. One kid is screaming for reasons unknown. The other one is pulling on your shirt or tugging on your arm, trying to show you something, even though they showed you something literally five seconds ago. The TV is blaring in an attempt to get the kiddos to leave you alone, but no one is watching it. Oil jumps from the pan and stings your hand. The microwave beeps.

You never want to see or hear or touch anything ever again. You wish you could fall into a void where you didn't even exist.

This, my friend, is overstimulation. And while all kinds of people can get overstimulated, parents are especially prone to it because kids are, well, overstimulating. They're loud and sticky and always there. We love them dearly, and at the same time, they're a lot.

This is especially true if you happen to have an AuDHD kiddo (pretty likely, seeing as both autism and ADHD are genetic) who is sensory seeking. They may run into you, grab you, yell nonsense sounds at you, all in an attempt to connect with you through sensory input.

Meanwhile, if you're more sensory avoidant, you may feel like the world is closing in on you with all this stimulation.

How can you meet your kids' needs, take care of the basics, like making dinner, and also meet your own needs?

It can feel totally impossible, and to a certain extent, maybe it is. But I believe there are ways we can lessen our overstimulation.

First, admit that you have sensory needs. Stop trying to just white-knuckle your way through, as though you're neurotypical. You're not, so stop pretending you are and start addressing your needs as if they're real and they matter. Because they do.

If you're especially sensitive to sound, wear earplugs or noise-canceling headphones around the house whenever you can. If you're super sensitive to touch, create a system where your kids can get your attention with either no or minimal physical contact (waving, saying a keyword, flashing the lights, etc.).

Second, do the same thing with your kids' needs. Come up with solutions that they can implement on their own (if they're old enough) when you're busy or feeling overwhelmed. Install a sensory swing they can use while you cook. Give them some headphones that play their preferred music. Let them snack on something stimulating, like Pop Rocks.

But also, be sure to set time aside where you feel regulated enough to connect with them through sensory input. Make sure there's time for snuggles, singing, wrestling, chasing, and more.

Finally, don't be afraid to simplify things so that they're less overstimulating. Feel free to make simple dinners if the bland flavor profile will cause you less overwhelm (this will also help with executive dysfunction, which we'll touch on in one of the following sections). It's okay to exclusively make CrockPot meals with those plastic liners so that there's fewer dishes, because let's be honest, washing and drying dishes is often a sensory nightmare.

It's okay to make things simpler on yourself. Just because you *can* push yourself further and do more doesn't mean you *have* to. You are not obligated to operate at 100 percent capacity all the time.

Boundaries and discipline

Something my husband and I say to each other over and over when our kids are testing our patience is "Hey, their job is to test the boundaries. Our job is to set them."

Sure, that sounds pretty simple, but in practice? It's damn near impossible, especially for AuDHD parents.

One of the biggest issues AuDHD parents face is often a lack of good modeling from our own parents. Until the last decade or so, autism and ADHD were both seriously underdiagnosed, and more often than not, AuDHD kids were not offered support or accommodation. Instead, they were met with invalidation and told to "toughen up" and "pay attention."

Even if your parents meant well and genuinely wanted to help, there were significantly fewer resources for parents of autistic and ADHD kiddos in the past compared to now.

In order to set healthy, helpful boundaries with our kids, many AuDHD parents must become cycle breakers. We have to look carefully at our own experiences growing up and make conscious decisions about which behaviors and dynamics we want to pass on, and which ones we don't. We often can't parent based on what feels "natural" because we might be used to some pretty unhealthy dynamics, like enmeshment (where the identities of each individual family member are dependent upon other members, and no one is allowed to be their own person) or triangulation (where person A has a problem with person B, but instead of talking to person B directly, person A talks to a totally different person, person C, and expects them to convey their message to person B for them).

And when our natural tendencies aren't the ones we want to act on, it's easy to feel like a terrible parent.

Like, who am I to raise human beings if my natural parenting instincts are "wrong"? What does it say about me if my first thought when there's conflict is to yell at or even spank my kids?

Here's what I think it says about us: we were raised in an environment that wasn't always a good fit for us, even if everyone involved was trying their best. Our needs often weren't met, and as a result, we don't always know how to meet our kids' needs either.

There's a popular saying on the internet that goes "Your first thought is what society told you to think. Your second thought is what you really think."

I like that, and feel like it applies well here. It's okay if your gut reaction isn't what you want it to be. That's just what you were programmed to do.

The real question is: what are you actually doing? Are you actually yelling, or do you just want to?

While I understand the mental pain caused by constantly wanting to scream and trying not to, there's still a big difference between that and actually flying off the handle all the time, especially from your kids' perspective.

So, what can you do to parent a little more calmly? First, I highly recommend silly singing. When you feel like you're about to scream, start singing a silly tune about how much you love your kids. I have personally used this many times, and it almost immediately diffuses the tension.

The next strategy I use to keep my cool actually goes back to the previous section on overstimulation. If I can keep the house attuned to my sensory needs, I find I'm much more capable of handling interpersonal stress.

But what if you're not really the yelling type? What if your issue with boundaries and discipline isn't accidentally being too harsh, but accidentally being too lenient?

I have spoken to many AuDHDers who also struggle with being overly permissive parents. Again, this is okay. It's not a sign that you're a horrible person or anything. In many cases, AuDHD parents allow their kids to get away with poor behavior, like hitting them, screaming at them, or refusing to listen to them, because it's simply easier than putting up a fight.

And hey, we've all been there.

But generally speaking, we don't want it to become a consistent pattern because kids flourish with boundaries and consequences, as long as they make sense for both you and them.

I think AuDHDers are particularly prone to this parenting style because we're often so exhausted by everything else, from our sensory environment to all the executive functioning demands in our lives, that we just can't find the energy to cope with one more thing.

Plus, you might be prone to permissive parenting if your own parents were permissive, or maybe even if your parents were needlessly strict. In an attempt to break the cycle and be gentler, we can swing too far in the other direction and become overly permissive.

It's such a fine line, parenting with kindness and firmness. Many AuDHDers struggle with finding the middle ground in all kinds of situations, and parenting is no different. We are prone to all-or-nothing thinking, which can lead to perfectionism in how we parent or even the expectations we have for our kids.

We're either the best parent ever or the worst. Our kids are either bundles of joy or minions of misery. We expect our kids to act like mini adults, or we let them be totally out of control. And worst of all, we often know we're swinging from one extreme to the next, and we know it's not good for us or for our kids. But we just don't know how to stop.

Look, I'm definitely not a parenting expert. But I know a lot about AuDHD, so here are some of my favorite strategies for finding the middle ground whenever my brain is trying to drive me to one extreme or another.

- **Wise mind journaling:** This strategy comes from Dialectical Behavioral Therapy (DBT), which emphasizes that neither your emotions nor your logic are better than the other. Instead, they're meant to work together in what DBT calls "wise mind." My way of doing this is by opening a journal to two blank pages. On the left, I write down how I feel. No holding back, just raw emotion, no matter how dramatic or even mean it might be. Then on the right-hand side, I write down the facts of the situation. We're talking the kind of stuff you could submit as evidence in a courtroom. Then I just sit back and read them both.

  More often than not, I find that my emotions do make

sense given the facts, even if they're a bit bigger than they might be for other people. Plus, when I look at the emotions and facts side by side, it's easier to find a middle ground between them. It's super clear, looking at them totally separated, that they don't make sense on their own. That I need both logic and emotion in order to make sense of anything.

- **Us vs. the problem:** Whenever I'm tempted to tell my kid he's grounded forever, I do whatever I can to remember that in all things, it's us vs. the problem, not me vs. my kid. My kid is never the problem. Even when he's doing something wrong, *he* isn't a problem—the behavior is. Once I remember that, I calm down pretty quickly because the issue becomes less about who we are as people and more about what we can do to solve a problem.

- **Therapy and/or coaching:** While I fully support being vulnerable and honest with your kiddos, there are some things they just don't need to hear, not until they're older, or maybe not at all. But that doesn't mean you don't have the right to feel or think those things. And you deserve an outlet for those thoughts and feelings, whether they're embarrassing or mean-spirited or shameful. Therapy and coaching can be a great way to feel heard without hurting your kids with your words.

Executive dysfunction

Being a parent also means being a household manager, and it only gets more complicated as they get older and get involved in sports or the school play or an after-school job. You have to keep track of who needs to be where, and when, and then you have to actually shuttle everyone everywhere, buy the supplies they need, whether it's school supplies or medication, and just generally be all-knowing and all-doing.

It's freaking exhausting for even the most organized among us, and, let's face it, AuDHDers are usually not very naturally organized.

"But Megan!" you cry, outraged. "That's not fair! I'm the most organized person I know!"

To which I can't help but wonder, are you organized because you like organization, or because you feel like your whole life would fall apart without it? Is your organization driven by what feels natural and easy, or driven by anxiety about things slipping through the cracks, almost as if you're naturally forgetful and disorganized, and use excessive organization as a compensation mechanism?

Sorry if that's a bit of a callout, but compensatory behaviors are a huge part of AuDHD. We might appear organized—heck, we might even actually be organized, but it requires a lot more time and energy for us than it would for a neurotypical person.

This is often due to executive dysfunction. We struggle to know what needs to get done, to intuitively understand how to do it most efficiently, and then to actually, y'know, do it all.

Basically, we have a hard time from start to finish. From organizing our thoughts to making a plan to executing that plan, executive dysfunction disrupts all of it. That is obviously hard on anyone, but it can be especially tricky with kids. After all, if your executive dysfunction causes you to miss an appointment, that's a pain, but if your executive dysfunction causes you to forget to pick your kid up from practice, and you lost your phone so the coach can't even call you to let you know, that's, like, a *big* problem.

I'm still learning how best to keep an organized household as an AuDHDer with major executive dysfunction, but here are some of my favorite hacks:

- If you have a partner(s), sync your calendars so you can stay updated on what the other is planning and coordinate. My husband and I used to double-schedule ourselves all the time before we did this. Now, it almost never happens.

- Put everything in that calendar as soon as you know about it. Never, ever assume you'll remember it later. You won't. Seriously, just put it in the calendar right away. Oh, and make sure you have reminders set up. I know reminders are easy to ignore a lot of the time, but I also know reminders have saved me from missing some very important meetings and appointments.

- Get your kids a visual schedule for their morning and bedtime routines. I know every kid ever seems to be utterly shocked and appalled by the reality of bedtime every single night, and we've found that the visual schedule helps a bit. Our kiddo enjoys checking the schedule and feeling a sense of accomplishment as he does each thing, instead of feeling dread about having to go to sleep. Plus, this will help you remember what your kid needs to do! Any time you can pull something out of your brain and rely on visual reminders instead, it can help reduce the mental load of household management.

- Get a meal prep service if you can afford it. My husband and I used Hello Fresh for a while, but you can try Blue Apron, Green Chef, or whatever meal service you like. Not having to go grocery shopping and having clear instructions and pre-measured ingredients was literally incredible. The one and only reason we've stopped is because of finances, but let me tell you, the moment we can afford it again, we're doing it again. It takes cooking from a task that eats up tons of energy and focus, to a task I can basically do on autopilot.

- If you have a partner(s), make sure coaches and teachers

have their phone number as well as yours. Even if your partner(s) is also AuDHD, at least by having both phone numbers, there's a better chance they can get hold of *someone*, even if one of you loses your phone or oversleeps.

As you can see, daily life as an AuDHDer is pretty different from daily life as a neurotypical. You're not imagining it; things really are probably harder for you in a lot of ways. But that doesn't mean there aren't solutions we can find together.

EXERCISES

➔ For three days, try to write down every single thing you do. It'll be a pain in the moment, but I can pretty much guarantee that when you look at everything you wrote, you'll have a new-found appreciation for how hard you're actually working and you'll give yourself a little credit.

➔ List out five more areas of daily life that your autism and ADHD affect on a regular basis. Then, for each section, list out the three biggest problems you experience, and then brainstorm three possible solutions for each problem.

➔ If you're feeling overwhelmed by just how all-encompassing your AuDHD is, go back to Chapter 2: Making Sense of Who You Are. Toward the end of the chapter, there's a section on how to find a good therapist, coach, or other helping professional who can help you sift through your overwhelm.

KEY TAKEAWAYS

→ Autism and ADHD affect so much more than just school and work. They affect every aspect of our daily lives as well.

→ Treat yourself like a houseplant. Your needs are neutral, and you deserve to be taken care of. Not because of anything you've done or accomplished, but simply because you exist. That's enough.

→ Whenever you're experiencing conflict with your partner(s), kids, or other loved ones, remember, it's not you vs. them—it's all of you vs. the problem. You're on each other's team!

CHAPTER 4

How to Succeed at Work

From Getting the Job to Keeping It to Actually Liking What You Do

I have to start this chapter with a huge disclaimer, which is that I have never held a traditional 9-5 job.

I've freelanced and taught college classes and worked in food service and run my own business, but I've never had an office job, except for a part-time gig one summer when I was 22.

This is actually a pretty common story amongst AuDHDers. Studies show that 85 percent of autistic folks are unemployed, while approximately 20 percent of those of us who are employed hold non-traditional employment.[1] And for ADHDers, 8 percent of us are unemployed[2] and we are nearly twice as likely to be entrepreneurs than our non-ADHD counterparts.[3]

For reference, folks without autism or ADHD have an unemployment rate of 3.6 percent in the United States[4] and around only about 7 percent of the general population (worldwide) are entrepreneurs.[5]

All of this is to say, this chapter isn't exactly going to be a how-to guide on climbing the corporate ladder. But it will be a guide on how to make ends meet, survive, and maybe even thrive and enjoy what you do.

What kind of job works best for AuDHDers?

This is such a popular question, and such a hard one to answer. Why? Because AuDHDers, especially autistic folks, are very diverse.

Studies show that scans of neurotypical brains are very similar to one another, but autistic brains? Each one shows huge differences, not just from neurotypical brains, but from other autistic brains as well.[6]

This means the saying that if you've met one autistic person, you've met ONE autistic person, is incredibly true. It's hard to generalize about autistic folks because we are all so different.

So I've decided to break this part of the book into sections based on two things: fulfillment factors and burnout triggers.

Fulfillment factors are aspects of a job that make you feel, well, fulfilled. Happy. Satisfied with your work in some way, therefore making that job a good fit in some ways. And burnout triggers are aspects of a job that can lead to burnout, therefore making that particular job (or at least doing it that particular way or with those particular people) a bad fit in some ways.

We'll explore some potential fulfillment factors to consider when looking for a job, then we'll take a look at some burnout triggers that should be avoided when possible, and then we'll combine this information into some specific job recommendations.

Fulfillment factors

Helping others

One possible reason someone might feel fulfilled by their job is knowing that their hard work is making someone else's life better in some way. It can be gratifying to know that you aren't just making your boss rich, but you're making other people happier, or helping them with things they find challenging, or saving them time or money somehow.

Many people would love it if they could help others with their job, but I also want to point out that this isn't as important to some folks, and that's 100 percent okay too. Your fulfillment factors are yours, and they don't have to look any one particular way.

Structure-to-novelty ratio

Everyone needs a combination of both structure and novelty, but this is especially true for AuDHDers. The autistic part of our brain might want all structure, all the time, and the ADHD part of our brain might only engage in our work if it's fun and new, so it's really important for many of us to find a job with a good structure-to-novelty ratio.

This ratio will be different for every AuDHDer, but here's a good rule of thumb: if what you do is the same day in and day out, you'll need some variety in the content of that work. And if the content of your work is the same every day, you'll need variety in how you're engaging with that content.

For example, if you're a freelance writer, you might be doing the same thing, writing, every day. But the specific topic you're writing about might shift from day to day. However, if you're a teacher, you might be teaching on the same topic all schoolyear, but each class period is totally different because there are different students with different questions and interests.

Good coworkers

This is a hard one to control, but it's undeniably a fulfillment factor for many. Although some autistic folks might not care too much about coworkers, and in fact would prefer to have little to no contact with them and just focus on doing their work, other autistic folks thrive in environments where they have great relationships with their coworkers. Especially if you've ever worked retail or food service, you know that who you're working with can make or break a shift.

Passion

For some people, passion for your work is essential for feeling fulfilled at work. For others, it's not such a big deal. In my opinion, AuDHDers are more likely to want to be passionate about their work for a few reasons.

First, boredom is literally painful for ADHDers in a way that it's just not for non-ADHDers. So, being passionate about our work decreases boredom and makes the job much more doable. Second, one thing autism and ADHD actually have in common is something called monotropic thinking.[7]

Monotropism is a fascinating topic, but to boil it down to its basics, the theory of monotropism, developed by Dinah Murray, Mike Lesser, and Wendy Lawson in 2005, says that attention is a finite resource, not something we can draw on endlessly.[8] And because it's finite, we have to strategize how to get the most out of the attention we have.

Polytropic thinkers (typically neurotypical folks) tend to use attention like a lantern. Their attention goes in many directions, participates in many ideas at once, but doesn't go too terribly deep with any one particular thing.

Monotropic thinkers, often including autistic folks, ADHDers, people with OCD, and more, tend to think more like a flashlight. We focus on one thing very deeply.

Because of this monotopic thinking style, AuDHDers are more likely than non-AuDHDers to feel much more fulfilled by a job they're passionate about because it allows us to really dig into our passion in one long tunnel, rather than being pulled in a million different, uninteresting directions.

Burnout triggers

Long hours

This one may differ based on your particular flavor of AuDHD, but many autistic folks especially tend to struggle with long hours. The florescent lights and small talk and sound of the air conditioner might be minor annoyances at 9am, but by 5pm, they can be truly untenable.

Additionally, ADHDers may struggle to stay focused for a full workday, especially as even the extended-release stimulant medications rarely last a full eight hours.

Detail-oriented work

Now, plenty of autistic folks love detail-oriented work, but ADHDers? Not so much, usually. Having to work with details all day every day can be utterly exhausting, painfully boring, and a highway to burnout. I mean, it's literally in the DSM criteria for diagnosing ADHD that we struggle to pay close attention to small details and often make all kinds of mistakes when it comes to dealing with minutae. So, when you're AuDHD, how you handle detail-oriented work will really depend on your unique presentation of AuDHD traits.

If you love detail-oriented work, but tend to shy away from big picture stuff, then I recommend becoming known around your workplace as "the detail person." Make it a valuable skill, rather than something that might hold you back. Remember that the big picture is built on details and you offer something incredibly valuable.

If you're absolutely not a detail person, like me, then I have two recommendations. First, if at all possible, get an assistant who can do the detail work for you. I know this isn't an option for a lot of people, but for many others, it is. Don't stop yourself from getting the help you need because you're embarrassed you can't do the detail work. We all have our own unique strengths, and it's okay if yours just isn't details.

Second, if that's not an option, then try to tap into your monotropic thinking and get all the details done in one go. If you do half the work one day, then take two days off and try to come back to it, you might have no idea where you left off or not remember how you did what you were doing. Instead, I recommend getting into a flow and getting it all done at once. Then, when it's done, ask a trusted coworker to go over it and look for mistakes.

Dedication to hierarchies

Because AuDHDers tend to struggle to perceive, understand, and respond "appropriately" to social cues, we often have a hard time with social hierarchies. Sometimes we perceive them, but don't agree with them, and other times we literally aren't sure who's supposedly "higher up" than someone else.

Many AuDHDers find it very challenging to operate within a structure that has a devoted dedication to hierarchies, where you can get in major trouble for going to the wrong person with the wrong thing (AKA going "over someone's head" or "bothering a higher-up with something small" or even just being friends with people in the "wrong" place in the hierarchy). Whether we are intentionally disregarding the hierarchy or simply not perceiving it at all, we are considered by others to be disrespectful, which can limit our tenure at these kinds of places of employment.

Emotional intensity

You've probably heard that ADHDers thrive in a crisis because, finally, the world around us reflects the chaos going on in our brains. And there's absolutely some truth to that, but what doesn't always get mentioned when people discuss this concept is the consequences that come later. For example, an ADHDer might keep a shockingly cool head during an intense situation, but once that situation resolves, they may get stuck in crisis mode, unable to relax. Or, especially if they're AuDHD, they might completely shut down or even dissociate after the crisis.

This means that if you're AuDHD and feel most fulfilled when doing emotionally intense work, you'll just have to do a lot of self-care after work. If that's okay with you, then this burnout trigger might not be such a big deal, but for other AuDHDers, this trigger can be a huge problem that's just too difficult to cope with.

Job recommendations

Helping professional

I can't tell you the number of ADHD, autistic, and AuDHD people I know who are nurses, therapists, coaches, or other helpers. The helping professions check a lot of the fulfillment factor boxes, such as helping others and lots of novelty within a set structure, and for many it is also a passion.

However, it's important to note that helping others is often emotionally intense, which can be difficult for AuDHDers since we tend to struggle with emotional regulation even without being in a dysregulating environment for work.

Whether or not a helping profession is right for you will likely come down to how your autism and ADHD present and your capacity to cope with emotionally intense situations.

Self-employment

From being an influencer to freelancing, working for yourself is a very real job, and one that can be an excellent choice for

AuDHDers. As a content creator myself, I am definitely partial to this one, but I will be totally honest, it's not right for everyone.

Working for yourself often comes with tons of novelty, flexible hours, and best of all for many of us? No annoying coworkers. Plus, you get to decide what you create content about, meaning you can focus on your passions.

However, there is very little structure built into self-employment. You have to create structure yourself, which, for many ADHDers, can be very difficult.

Also, even though you don't have coworkers, you will likely have to work with brands, clients, or other entrepreneurs. In some ways, this is easier than traditional workplace social interactions because you get to choose which ones you want to engage with, but it can also be harder, because the rules are even less clear.

Self-employment isn't right for all AuDHDers, but it's a very real option for many of us.

Tradesperson

I know it's super vague for me to say "tradesperson," but I've seen so many AuDHDers succeed as plumbers, mechanics, painters, and pretty much every other trade.

Many tradespeople (once they're no longer an apprentice, anyway) have a lot of control over their schedule, which is great for AuDHDers with inconsistent energy levels. Many trades have rigid structures in place around how things are to be done, but what you do day in and day out often covers a wide range, allowing for a good structure-to-novelty ratio.

However, it's important to consider that some tradespeople don't get much novelty in their work. A welder might weld the same type of pieces together over and over all day. A painter might get pretty bored painting an entire house the same "greige" (gray + beige) color. Additionally, tradespeople often work long hours, and some tradespeople work outside in the sun, which can be tricky for autistic folks, as many of us are very heat-sensitive.

Our society puts a lot of value on traditional 9–5 desk jobs, and those jobs are incredibly valuable, but our homes and offices and cars wouldn't work without tradespeople. Don't avoid these jobs just because they sometimes garner less respect. They often pay very well and, in my experience, tend to be even more accommodating of disability than office jobs are.

How to get a job

Okay, Megan, you say, there are jobs out there that might work with my brain. But how in the world am I supposed to actually get a job when I can't even make it through a conversation without royally screwing something up?

First, let's reframe that thought. Yes, you communicate differently. And yes, sometimes that leads to awkwardness or discomfort or miscommunication. But you're not "screwing up"—you're trying your best and that should be acknowledged. Try thinking something a little kinder, like "How am I supposed to get a job when it feels like my communication style is on a different radio frequency than most employers?"

This gentler approach is better because it allows you to be nicer to yourself, but it also opens up possibilities for accommodation. If the problem is that you're on a different frequency, then the solution is to get on the same frequency.

You can do this by specifically searching for jobs that operate primarily using your preferred mode of communication, or you can work on your skills in communicating on the employer's frequency.

Tips for communicating with employers

Here's the thing about many neurotypical folks: they often feel awkward when being direct. So they approximate their meaning, they stretch 70 percent of the way across the chasm toward you, and they expect you to fill in the gaps and stretch the other 30 percent of the way.

This is not how most autistic folks communicate. We tend to just give 100 percent of the info, that way you know precisely what we're thinking and feeling. Giving anything less feels like being intentionally obscure, which doesn't feel helpful to us.

But for many neurotypicals, giving 100 percent of the information feels overwhelming, maybe even condescending or rude, so they give bits and pieces.

If you want to communicate more clearly with potential employers, I encourage you to ask questions. Lots of them. Sure, some potential employers won't appreciate this, but let's be honest, if you do get the job, you'll likely have lots of questions, maybe more than the typical employee. Do you really want a job where you're ignored, shamed, or even punished for asking for clarification or assistance?

Probably not. So, in the interview process, ask your questions. You should ask questions that you genuinely want to know the answer to, but in case you're drawing a blank, here are some types of questions I've asked in the past:

- **Ask something about the topic of the job.** For instance, when I was writing freelance articles about acne, I asked about the target audience and the tone I was expected to write in. In my experience, most employers enjoy talking about the topic of their work and enjoy these kinds of questions.

- **Ask why the interviewer likes working there.** This is a great vibe check to see if the company treats their people well. If the person flounders or gives you a non-answer, it may not be the best work environment. On the other hand, if they immediately jump in with what they love about it, the company may put a lot of emphasis on keeping their employees happy.

- **Ask about the previous employee in this position.** What did the company like about them, what made them successful, and if they're able to share, why did they move on to something different? These questions can give you a sneak peek into what they expect from someone in this role, and you can see if you'd be a good fit. If they describe a person who is totally opposite to you and they're just gushing over how much they loved the previous person, you might find yourself in a bit of an awkward fit.

In my experience with freelancing, my clients loved how many questions I asked. To them, it showed that I cared about their project and wanted to do a good job. This is how a good employer will respond to lots of questions.

Second, if you're in the interview and you're not sure if you're on the same wavelength, just check in. Let them know that you understood their words to mean XYZ, and ask if that's correct, or if they had other intentions that you missed.

Again, this will let them know you're invested in the position and the interview conversation, rather than just doing whatever you can to land the job and get paid.

Finally, in the interview, please feel free to lie.

I know, I know, for many autistic folks, this goes against everything we feel in our bones. I mean, the entire *point* of communication is to let others know what you're thinking and feeling, so why even bother to communicate if you're not going to tell the truth?

Well, an interview isn't a normal conversation. It's a negotiation. They want your skills and work hours, and you want their money and security. And many employers, even the relatively good ones, are willing to lie or fudge the truth a bit in an interview. They may say their budget for the position is $60,000 a year, when they know they could offer up to $95,000 a year. They may say they love hiring working mothers, when, in reality, their workplace is incredibly hostile to pregnant folks and parents. They can lie about all kinds of things.

While many folks wouldn't consider withholding information to be lying, for many autistic folks, we do view this as lying. After all, if a company says they do not allow their employees to work remotely, but then after you get hired, you find out that several of your coworkers negotiated to work from home 50 percent of the time, that feels an awful lot like a lie. We were told that was off the table, so we respected that boundary. But in job negotiations, the boundaries that the company states are often flexible, if not a genuine lie.

While I don't encourage folks to lie in their interpersonal relationships, I do believe it can be beneficial, and even sometimes necessary, in job negotiations.

Don't tell them you only need $65,000 a year to cover your bills; tell them you really need $80,000. Planning on getting pregnant? No need to disclose that to them (especially because it's actually illegal for them to ask you about that, in the United States, anyway).

If it helps, remember that you are an individual person negotiating with a company. The power dynamics are already stacked against you. Use whatever tools or leverage you can to get a good job, with good pay, that works with your brain.

To disclose, or not to disclose

Oh man, this is such a huge question in the world of disability. Here are the arguments:

Some folks argue that you should disclose your AuDHD during the interview process for three main reasons:

- They know they'll struggle to actually do the job if they also have to monitor themselves to not "look autistic" or not "act ADHD."
- They want or need accommodations from the job in order to do it, and they think the only way to get those accommodations is through disclosure (hint: this is not always the case!).
- They have undergone an unmasking journey and refuse to hide their identity anymore. Period.

Other folks argue that you absolutely should *not* disclose your AuDHD during the interview process for three main reasons:

- There's not time in an interview to explain the intricacies of autism and ADHD, so the employer will fill in the blanks with stereotypes and stigma that won't help you get the job. It's illegal to discriminate based on disability status, but it still happens all the time.
- In many places of employment, you can implement many accommodations by simply asking for them, without explaining why you need them, and many employers will say yes. This makes disclosure unnecessary for many folks.
- It makes more sense to disclose later, after they've gotten to know you as a human being first and their understanding of you will help override some of their misconceptions about autism and/or ADHD.

Personally, I don't have much of a choice. My whole career at this point is talking about my autism and ADHD on the internet. One quick Google search will out me real quick. And for me, that's okay. I've spent much of my life hiding my true self, and I'm happy to let go of any opportunity that requires me to keep hiding.

But I know that's a hugely privileged position to hold. I can only say that because my husband has a steady job in insurance. I can afford to be choosy about my job. I know that's not the case for many AuDHDers. If I had to hide my AuDHD to feed my babies, I would. And it's okay for you to do that too, if you need to.

Choosing to disclose or withhold your AuDHD at work is a very personal decision, but many of the other AuDHDers I've spoken to about this seem to agree that what's important is that you get the support you need to do your job well without burning out. At some companies, this is entirely possible without any official disclosure. You can simply mention that you work better with headphones or negotiate work-from-home time without explaining specifically why you need it.

However, other companies may require official paperwork in order to grant any accommodations at all, in which case, the decision to disclose becomes much more complicated. You don't want to burn out unnecessarily by not asking for accommodations that your company might happily provide with the proper documentation, but you also don't want to lose your job by disclosing to people who hold prejudice and stigma against autism and ADHD.

One solution to this problem could be to withhold your diagnoses in the interview, and once you get the acceptance email, to reply by saying that you're thrilled about the position, but before you accept, you'd like to check if a few workplace accommodations might be appropriate. You can either explain why you need the accommodations, maybe even providing links to your favorite autism and ADHD educational resources just to make sure they're on the same page as you, or you can simply ask for the accommodations without an explanation. If the company mentions any neuro-affirming practices on their website, as more and more companies are starting to do, be sure to mention those in this email too so you can gently remind them that what you're asking for is in line with what they say their mission is.

At the end of the day, no one can tell you whether to disclose, or when or how to do it. But I feel like I have to say this: my life is better because I'm open about my AuDHD with everyone, including the people I work with. I know there's a lot of privilege in that, but it would be dishonest if I didn't tell you how happy I am that I don't have to worry about who knows about my AuDHD and keep secrets. It's just one less burden on my mind, and I'm glad for it.

How to like your job

Okay, let's assume you survive the interview and get the job. What then?

Because let's face it, no matter how neuro-affirming the job is, there are likely going to be some aspects that are hard for you to cope with. So, let's talk about how to maximize your enjoyment of your job. We spend about 35 percent of our days working (assuming you work only one job, with no overtime). Let's not be miserable 35 percent of the time.

Sensory accommodations

Let's go over the eight main senses and how you can accommodate sensory differences at work for each one.

- **Sight:** If your work utilizes bright fluorescent lights, try wearing blue light blocking glasses, or even sunglasses if necessary. If you have a cubicle, decorate it to suit your sensory needs. Personally, I'm a sensation seeker, visually, so my desk looks like a rainbow threw up on it. That works for me. Do whatever works for you.

- **Sound:** Invest in a good pair of noise-canceling headphones or earbuds, if you work in a place where you don't need to hear in order to be safe. If you can't shut out all the noise, try something like Loop ear plugs, which block some noise, but not all.

- **Taste:** Pack your safe foods every day—the foods that you enjoy and don't give you the ick. If the air in your place of work tastes strange (happens a lot in trade work, like painting or carpentry), make sure you've got long-lasting, flavorful gum.

- **Smell:** If your place of work smells odd, ask your office mates if it's alright for you to bring in a candle, a diffuser, or one of those things that plugs into the wall. If that doesn't work, dab a small amount of a pleasant scent under your nose, above your lips, periodically throughout the day to help mask the unpleasant smell.

- **Touch:** Dress as comfortably as you can while still wearing something appropriate for your place of work. Especially the shoes! If you work at a desk, make sure your chair is comfortable. If you work outside, wear sunscreen religiously, because sunburn is a sensory nightmare.

- **Proprioception** (awareness of your body in space): Get soft covers to put on the corners of your desk if you know you tend to cut corners and hit the crap out of your hips and legs. If you crave proprioceptive input, try lifting weights before work, and getting a desk chair that swivels.

- **Interoception** (awareness of your internal experiences): Set alarms to remind you to eat, drink water, and use the restroom. Try to make a work friend who invites you to eat with them, so you don't forget.

- **Vestibular:** Take the stairs if the elevator makes you dizzy. If you work at home, take regular dance breaks throughout the day. Go for a walk on your lunch break if you have a primarily sedentary job, and sit or lie down on your lunch break if you have a physically demanding job.

Gamification

When in doubt, make it a game.

My mom taught me this from a young age, when I would drag my feet picking up toys. She'd encourage me to see how fast I could pick them up, or to pretend the floor was lava and see how I could get around the living room to pick up without stepping in the lava. Somehow, games make unpleasant work manageable.

Creativity craves constriction. The ADHD brain naturally goes in about a million different directions, so when you force it to go only one or two ways, it's a challenge. It's unnatural. It's fun.

Here are some ways I gamify my work:

- **Bingo.** When I feel overwhelmed by my to-do list, I make a nine-grid Bingo board, fill in nine things from my to-do list, and then I try to get one Bingo. I don't have to do all nine things—I just have to get three in a row somehow. It makes a large number of tasks feel less daunting.

- **Roll a D20.** I love Dungeons & Dragons, and I love collecting dice to play D&D. So, again, when I have a huge to-do list, I'll write out 20 things that need doing and number them, and then I'll roll a 20-sided dice, and I'll do whatever to-do list item aligns with the number I rolled. Randomness is always a good way to motivate me.

- **Cosplaying as a productive person.** Cosplay is costume role play, and it's a shockingly effective way to get yourself into a productive mindset. Personally, I love Leslie Knope from *Parks and Recreation*, so I go to the store, buy a bunch of waffles, put on my favorite (AKA only) blazer, and get to work.

Body doubling

If you haven't heard of body doubling, you are missing out, friend. It's simple: when two or more people are trying to be productive together, in person or virtually, they all get more productive.

For any science nerds out there, it's like a covalent bond. Just like how two atoms can share an electron, two people can share productive vibes.

I often body double with my friend who lives nearby, my husband, or even my kiddo, but if you're more isolated, you can actually body double in some other creative ways. For example, did you know there are YouTube videos where people film themselves working for hours? You can play those and body double with them. Even though they aren't live, it still works pretty well.

I also recommend checking out my community, The Neurodivergent Clubhouse,* which features body doubling three times per week in a variety of time zones, or other coworking services that match you up with strangers who also want to be productive, like FocusMate** or CaveDay.***

I have found that body doubling is hugely effective for nearly

*   www.theneurocuriosityclub.com/nd-clubhouse
**   www.focusmate.com
*** www.caveday.org

all ADHDers and most AuDHDers, but it may be less effective for autistic folks. This is because being around other people can cause the urge to mask to kick in, and masking is inherently draining and distracting, and often makes us less productive.

If body doubling with real people doesn't work for you, try body doubling with a stuffed animal, or with a video from your favorite YouTube creator, or with a pretend, invisible camera crew, like you're in *The Office*.

Making work friends

This one is so hard, but if you can swing it, it can make work much more fun.

Even as an entrepreneur who works for myself, I need work friends. Doing your work all alone, with no one to vent to or celebrate with, is very lonely for many of us. But as an AuDHDer, you probably struggle with making friends (more on this in the next chapter). I know my relationships with work friends have been very hit or miss.

Sometimes we seem so close, and then I slowly realize there's a separate group chat that includes everyone but me. Other times, they just ghost me, disappearing no matter how many messages I send to check in to see if they're okay.

But every now and again, I've managed to find a work friend who is enthusiastic, like me, and inconsistent, like me, and doesn't just tolerate me but actually enjoys spending time with me.

And it makes work so much more fun, because I have someone to talk to about it. I know making work friends can be hard, but in my experience, it's often worth trying.

If you're looking for more work accommodations, I highly recommend checking out the Job Accommodation Network.*

---

*   www.askjan.org

EXERCISES

→ List some of your personal fulfillment factors. Why do you enjoy the things you enjoy?

→ Brainstorm jobs that incorporate your skills and could have similar motivations to why you enjoy other aspects of your life

→ List accommodations that would make a job more doable or enjoyable for you (with a list of examples for inspiration)

KEY TAKEAWAY

→ Your worth is not defined by your job, but if we can make work more enjoyable and sustainable, our quality of life often increases.

CHAPTER 5

You and Me and AuDHD

Navigating Neurodivergent Relationships

This chapter is not just about romantic relationships, so aromantic folks, don't skip this! We're going to talk about how to relate to other people in general, whether that's in a romantic way or a platonic way. Because autism and ADHD affect all aspects of our lives, not just school and work.

Our relationships are also impacted by our neurodivergence, in countless ways.

For example, when I first started unmasking around my partner, he felt like I'd been lying to him for years about who I really was, and we had to navigate what our relationship would look like with me showing up as my real self, and talk a lot about how masking wasn't an intentional lie, but rather a survival mechanism I was largely unaware of for a long time.

Or how it took over a decade for me to have an autistic meltdown in front of my best friend. I'd known her since we were 12, but it wasn't until I was 28 that I finally reached out for her help during a meltdown, because it took me that long to trust that she wouldn't judge me for losing control like that.

Connecting with others is hard. But it's possible. And it all starts with a good relationship with yourself.

Relationships with others build upon your relationship with yourself

Don't worry, this section won't repeat that horrible saying, "You need to love yourself before you can expect anyone else to love you."

That is the meanest possible way of saying, "We seek out the love we think we deserve, so the way we relate to ourselves is the baseline for the treatment we'll accept from others."

It's not a bad thing to struggle with self-worth and self-love. Our society doesn't want us loving ourselves, because if we did, we would never put up with fascism or capitalism or oppression of any kind.

So there's this undercurrent throughout everything in our world that says, "You're not enough."

This is especially true for people who have been historically (and currently) oppressed. In fact, the undercurrent tends to be much nastier to Black folks, disabled folks, trans folks, and more. It probably sounds more like "You're actually the problem here. If you disappeared, the world would be better."

This is not true. It is *not* true.

But we hear it all the time. We hear it in fatphobic novels that describe fat characters as "dumpy" or "disgusting," we hear it in legislation that prevents people who receive disability benefits from ever possessing more than $2000 in assets[1] and allowing for disabled workers to make pennies per day,[2] we hear it in the self-help world that claims to help us, while simultaneously telling us that our own lack of self-esteem is to blame for our relationship struggles.

How could you *not* have low self-esteem in this kind of world?

And how are you supposed to love yourself when no one else seems to love you?

I mean, love is a relational experience, and it's supposed to be modeled for us from a very young age, but many AuDHDers don't exactly receive the kind of support and nurturing that they need in childhood.

Without that fundamental foundation, how are we supposed to teach ourselves to love ourselves?

We need a blueprint. And for many of us, it starts with fiction.

How fictional characters shape our relationship with ourselves

If you don't have anyone in your real life to show you what love looks like, or if you have people who love you but don't get you, turn to fiction.

No, I'm so serious, this shit works.

Right now, I want you to write down five of your favorite fictional characters from books, movies, TV shows, video games, comic books—literally any fictional world. Pick the characters you really resonate with, the ones you come back to over and over, the ones you just...love.

Okay, now I want you to write down five qualities that each character possesses that you admire.

Now, go through and underline, highlight, or circle each quality that you also possess.

Finally, I want you to write down your favorites of the following statements:

- If I can admire these qualities in others, I must admire them in myself as well.
- If my life were a book, I would be someone's favorite character.
- Even one good quality is enough to redeem many villains. I have at least one good, redeeming quality.
- Some of my favorite characters are disabled. It's important

that these characters exist in books, and therefore it must be important that I exist in real life too.

- Even the best characters mess up. My mistakes don't preclude me from being lovable and good.

So many of us AuDHD folks turn to fiction when it becomes clear that we aren't fitting in among our peers. And I say lean into this. Allow those relationships with fictional characters to start healing the wounds that tell you that you're not enough.

Affirmations (with bridge thoughts)

Another great way to improve your relationship with yourself as an AuDHDer is affirmations, with the help of something called "bridge thoughts."

See, the main problem with affirmations, especially when you're autistic, is that you know it's nonsense. You can say "I'm a millionaire" in the mirror every day until you die, but if it's not true, it's not true.

So I recommend saying affirmations that feel true. How do we do this? By building a bridge between our current thought processes, which might be overwhelmingly negative or degrading, and the thoughts we'd much rather think, but feel unrealistic and out of reach.

For example, a few years ago, I was really struggling with the thought that I was unlovable. Just totally impossible for anyone to really, truly love me.

Oof, right?

The thought I wanted to think instead was "I'm so easy to love." But that felt like a lie. It was so false, I couldn't get behind it at all. In fact, trying to use that as an affirmation usually just made me sadder, because it felt so far from my reality.

But eventually, I found some more neutral thoughts in between "I'm unlovable" and "I'm easy to love."

I started with "I am not the devil" or "I am not possessed by a demon," which were things I absolutely worried about for a while there. Then I moved on to "I am human, like everyone else. I'm not better or worse than most people." Once that felt true, I tried out "I'm likable. People like me." Then it was "I'm lovable. People love me." And nowadays, I'm really working on the "I'm easy to love" thought. It still feels out of reach most days, but I know I'm getting there.

Now it's your turn. If I were to ask you how you feel about who you are as a person, what's the first thought that pops into your mind? This could be anything. Maybe your first thought is "I don't even know who I am." Maybe it's "I like myself, but I don't think I love myself." Don't judge what comes up—just write it down.

Then, if I asked you what your heart desperately wants to believe is true about you, what would you say then? Write that down too. Again, this could be anything from "I'm a helpful, honest, good human being" to "I'm not the worst person who's ever lived." No judgment.

Now find a more neutral thought in between those two. Make sure it feels at least 75 percent true. For some folks, that will be something as simple as "Someone loves me, even if it's not me." For other people, it might be something more like "I love myself sometimes, and that's good enough."

Write it down, and practice it every single day. Set an alarm on your phone, write it on your mirror, have a friend text it to you every morning—whatever you have to do to expose yourself to this bridge thought as much as possible.

Let's talk about friendship

Friendship is hard.

Okay, but it can also be super fun and fulfilling and life-giving. Personally, I think the joys of friendship are worth the risks. And believe me, I've had some painful friendship ghosting, breakups, and more.

Why do I still try to make and keep friends, when history tells me I'm generally very bad at it?

Because some of the friends I've managed to stay in contact with are some of the best, most supportive people I will ever meet, and I'm eternally grateful that I tried to be their friend, despite being bad at it. And I really, truly believe that there are even more amazing, supportive people out there, just waiting for us to stumble into each other's lives.

But that will never happen if I never try. So, let's talk about how to try to make friends as an adult with autism and ADHD.

How to make friends

Did you know that, on average, it takes approximately 200 hours of time together for people to consider themselves "good friends"?[3]

No wonder it's so much harder to make friends as an adult! In school, you spend eight hours a day sitting next to your peers, chatting between classes or working on group assignments together, then you hang out with people after school at extracurriculars or at a retail or fast food job. Plus, many of us grew up with siblings to go home to—our first friendships.

As a grown-up, you sit at a desk and stare at a screen for eight hours. If you have kids, you take care of them after work, and then, at 9pm, you finally get some time for yourself, so you turn on YouTube or scroll TikTok until it's time for bed.

When, exactly, are you supposed to be clocking 200 hours with people to make "good friends"?

If you spend two hours every single weekend with one person, it'll still take nearly two years for you to become "good friends" with them.

Compare that to being in school, where you might have two classes with someone, equating to about two hours. But that's two hours every day except weekends, so it would only take half a year to become "good friends."

And all of this isn't even taking into consideration all the autistic and ADHD barriers to making friends, which include:

- **The autistic struggle to understand social cues.** Like, apparently when someone asks about your favorite book, they don't actually care if it's precisely and definitively the best book you've ever read; they're really asking, "What kind of books do you like? Do we like the same kinds of books? Could we relate over books?" Many autistic folks I know, myself included, often struggle to start friendships because we try to answer small talk literally instead of using it as a social lubricant to get to the more fun parts of conversation.

- **The ADHD tendency to interrupt.** I can't tell you the number of conversations I've walked away from thinking, "Man, my throat is sore from talking so much; did I shut up at all? I don't think I let them talk more than five minutes total— why did I do that?" It's hard to make friends when you don't let them talk long enough to really get to know them.

- **The AuDHD tendency to overthink every social interaction.** Your autism doesn't understand what's going on. Your ADHD wants to perform so that no one notices how lost you are. You walk away from every interaction replaying the conversation in your head, picking it apart until you're convinced you screwed everything up and they'll never want to talk to you again. This mindset doesn't exactly make it easy or fun or likely that you'll reach out again.

You might even say no if they reach out, because you're so convinced they're only doing it out of pity or something.

So, with all these barriers in mind, how in the world do you make friends as an AuDHD adult???

Tip #1: Make online friends

There are autistic, ADHD, and AuDHD communities absolutely flourishing online right now. Join some Discord servers, hop into some Facebook groups, and start talking to people. Of course I recommend my Neurodivergent Clubhouse community, but many of the other creators listed in Resources for AuDHDers at the end of this book also have their own communities you can join. I recommend when you first join these groups, introduce yourself, but then lurk a bit. Get the feel for what people tend to post about, how honest and vulnerable they tend to be, and how unmasked you can safely be in this space.

I know, for me at least, it can be tempting to jump in and start posting all kinds of stuff. Maybe oversharing a bit or expecting to just skip that 200-hour "close friend" time requirement and jump into being besties with these people. But I tend to feel better and have more fun when I adjust my expectations and realize that even when you immediately click with someone, it still takes time to really trust them and become friends, rather than acquaintances.

Tip #2: Make a standing date with the friends you want to be closer to

What if you have lots of kinda sorta friends, but not many close friends? Well, then you gotta put in some hours. Create a standing date for coffee on Saturday mornings, or a walk together after daycare dropoff, or schedule a crafting night once a week.

Sure, it might take two years, but the years are going to pass anyway, right? Do you want to be two years older with a better, closer friend, or two years older in the same place with this friend as you were two years ago? Might as well try, right?

Tip #3: Spend more time in environments you enjoy

Do not go to bars if you hate bars. Even if you meet someone there you like, odds are, they will want to go to bars, and then you're either stuck going places you hate, or you lose the chance at friendship because you can't stand being in that environment.

Instead, spend more time in environments outside your house that you enjoy, and pay attention to other people who might be looking for a kindred spirit. This does not mean go bother people with headphones on (headphones are usually a sign a person would rather be alone right now). But look for other people who are just sitting at the coffee shop looking around, or people watching at the library, or sitting on a bench at the park.

I actually just made a new friend this way. I was at my favorite coffee shop when a woman walked in with a tiny, newborn baby. We chatted briefly about how old her baby was, and how old my kids were, then we went back to what we were doing. But before I got up to leave, I scrounged up all my courage and wrote down my phone number on a piece of paper and said, "Hey, I don't have a lot of mom friends around here, and I remember how hard those postpartum weeks are. Would you want to exchange numbers and, I don't know, maybe just get coffee together sometimes?"

I was so embarrassed. I sounded rambly and foolish and needy. She was going to awkwardly say yes and then never text me. I was absolutely kicking myself for doing this.

To my utter shock, her face lit up and she said, "Yes, oh my God, absolutely. Give me your number, I'll text you right now."

And now we text once or twice a week and have plans to get coffee soon.

Are we going to end up being besties? I don't know yet. But hey, not every relationship has to be a forever relationship. Sometimes people are in your life during a time when you both need each other, and that's okay. That's enough. Stop putting so much pressure on every relationship to be amazing right away. Sometimes things just start out with a spark and a "Yes, oh my God, absolutely."

How to keep friends

Raise your hand if you've ever had a friend reply to your messages slower and slower until they just...stop responding entirely.

Raise your hand if you've had a friend confront you about being a "bad" friend in some regard, usually for not reaching out enough or always turning down their invitations to go do things together.

Raise your hand if you've ever been part of a friend group that mysteriously does stuff without you sometimes, like the whole group except you, and it took you a ridiculously long time to realize they had a separate group chat without you?

Raise your hand for bonus points if, instead of realizing those people were not very kind, you forced your way into the other group chat.

Are you raising your hand? Yeah, me too.

Maintaining a healthy relationship with someone can be tricky for everyone, but there are some extra struggles that are specific to autistic and ADHD brains, like:

- **The ADHD tendency to literally forget about people if you don't see them all the time.** ADHDers have serious issues with object permanence, where if we can't see something (or someone), we know they still exist, but we lack reminders that tell us to reach out. This can result in inconsistent communication that others may read as uncaring.

- **The autistic struggle with going out.** Some autistic folks, especially those of us who are more sensory seeking, may love bars and clubs, but many other autistic folks who are more sensory avoidant may hate bars and clubs. So we turn down invitations to go out over and over until the other person assumes we don't like them or that we just aren't worth the effort to drag out of the house.

- **The energy inconsistencies that come with AuDHD.** Sometimes we have lots of energy and can do all the things, and other times, we're totally drained, maybe even burnt out, and can't do anything at all. If we tend to be more energetic around some people and less energetic around others, even if it's a total coincidence, the people we're more low-energy around might take it personally.

And all of this isn't even to mention the friendship struggles that can come with friendship trauma. Nearly every autistic, ADHD, and AuDHD person I know has some kind of significant friendship trauma. What I mean by friendship trauma is traumatic past events involving friends.

One of my friends had her best friends in the world ditch her for no apparent reason in middle school. They made a whole scene of it in the cafeteria.

Another one of my friends had her best friends refuse to attend her wedding because they thought she was veering from "God's plan" for her by marrying her husband.

And me? I guess my trauma comes from all the little things piling up. The sheer number of friends who have disappeared from my life for reasons I can't understand.

But despite all these barriers, I actually have a couple of incredibly good friends in my life.

Best friend since childhood

I've known my best friend since 6th grade when we somehow had the exact same class schedule, and we just became friends by default. It's been nearly two decades since that fateful first day of school, and I still call her when I'm bored, she still sends me memes, and we go to each other's kids' birthday parties. Do we talk consistently? No, of course not—we both have ADHD. But we're still the best of friends.

How have we stayed friends? I think it comes down to three main things:

- **We've grown together.** We've both changed radically since 6th grade. In some ways, we've grown in opposite directions, but in many other ways, we've grown in parallel. We didn't have rigid ideas of who the other one was supposed to be, so we've accepted one another for who we are, in every iteration.

- **We've fought.** Look, no two people are exactly the same, meaning any good relationship is going to have disagreements. If you shy away from that disagreement, you either get a huge blowup or a slow fizzling out. Instead, we've just...fought. We fight clean, no name-calling or anything like that, but we let the other one know when we disagree.

- **We text when things are good, bad, and in between.** We don't only reach out when we're celebrating or only when we're struggling. This can create a friendship that relies on toxic positivity, or relies on bad things happening to feel close. Instead, we talk through all of it.

Best friend since college

My second best friend I also technically knew since I was little. We were in the same Girl Scout troop all growing up, and we were both in the marching band together in high school, but it wasn't until we went to the same college and decided to room together that we really became close.

And now, 12 years after deciding to room together, we're still best friends. We lived together throughout all of college and in grad school, and eventually moved out of our last apartment together so I could go get married and live with my husband. I was thrilled to be with my husband after years of long-distance dating, but part of me really truly missed living with her.

Now, we live 20 minutes from each other and see each other all the time. How have we stayed friends? These are the three things I think make our friendship stronger:

- **We spend quality time together.** And for us, this can look like anything. Sometimes it's attending a workout class together, other times it's vegging and watching YouTube, and other times it's eating as much Mexican food as we can while drinking margaritas and laughing at stories we've told each other over and over.

- **We don't text all the time.** I think one of my favorite parts of this particular friendship is how we can pick up where we left off, no matter how long it's been since we talked last. Sure, we hang out quite a bit, but even when we don't, it's not like the friendship is fading at all. It'll always be there.

- **We validate each other.** Everyone needs that friend they can go to and say, "This is ridiculous, I'm being ridiculous, but please tell me I'm not," and their friend will say, "Girl, you have *every* right to feel this way." My Best Friend Since College is that friend for me.

Best friend in adulthood

I know, I know, a *third* best friend? You might be doubting my autism diagnosis at this point, but please remember, autistic folks can have friends! We just tend to make friends with other neurodivergent folks, or with extremely compassionate people who are happy to make room for our autism.

That is the case with my Best Friend in Adulthood. She is the kindest person I know, by far, and no one in my life who knows her would argue or be offended by that. She's just that kind.

We met in college and were close then, but we've just gotten closer and closer throughout adulthood, and I would absolutely consider her a best friend now. Here are three things that have strengthened our relationship over the years:

- **I encourage her to be angry, and she encourages me to be sad.** I know these are usually considered "negative" emotions, but both of us struggle to actually feel our feelings sometimes, and one of the best parts of my relationship with her is how we are able to open up the floodgates for each other.

- **We work together!** I know for some folks, this would be too blurry of a line, but for us, it really works. I spend a lot of my time and energy on work, and it's so great to have her as my virtual assistant because it means we have built-in time together.

- **We learn from each other.** We both really love learning, and both of us are full of fun facts. I never walk away from a conversation with her without learning something new, and she's always happy to let me infodump.

EXERCISES

→ On one side of the page, write exactly how you feel about a relationship situation, no holding back, then on the other side, write how you think reality might be, even if it's not totally in line with how you feel. Then on the bottom of the page, try to reconcile the two.

→ Think about one of your relationships and write down what accommodations you need in that relationship. Consider what accommodations the other person needs and write them down too.

KEY TAKEAWAY

→ Relationships are tricky when you're both autistic and ADHD, but that doesn't mean you're doomed to never have a good, healthy, happy relationship with anyone. Start on your relationship with yourself and build relationships with others upon that foundation.

To Mask or Not to Mask

Coping with Neurotypical Expectations

Masking is a survival strategy among autistic people, where we try to hide our natural way of connecting with the world and instead try to act like the people around us.

Many AuDHDers mask heavily and you'd never know they were autistic or ADHD, which is why when we finally get diagnosed and feel a tremendous sense of relief, we're so hurt when people say, "You couldn't be AuDHD! You're so normal!" We've spent our whole lives struggling, so when people say this, not only does it invalidate our current identity as an AuDHDer, it also invalidates our past struggles and shows us that no one has ever really, truly known us. This is profoundly lonely.

Other AuDHDers don't mask much or at all. Sometimes it's because they grew up in an accommodating environment where they didn't have to mask so much. Other times, it's because they've made the conscious decision not to mask, often after a serious burnout due to masking.

But in many cases, it's because the AuDHDer can't mask for whatever reason. Maybe they're non-speaking and they can't hide that. Maybe they don't perceive social cues to such an extent that they're unable to replicate them in order to mask. Maybe their executive dysfunction presents in a way that they have high support needs and cannot work or live alone safely.

Masking or not masking, neither one is better than the other. Each one presents its own unique challenges and comes with its own benefits. What makes masking or not masking so hard is when we feel we don't have any choice in the matter.

Many AuDHDers have their agency stripped away, not necessarily by individual neurotypical people, but by the broader neurotypical culture, more accurately called "neuronormativity,"[1] which is the idea that everyone should do everything the same way, that there is a correct way to live life and to be a person, that there is such a thing as a "normal" brain.

All of that is nonsense. We know this. But knowing that this is nonsense doesn't stop those expectations from existing, both within our society and within ourselves.

But before we explore how neuronormativity worms its way into our own brains, let's take a look at the influences that formed neuronormativity and the ways it presents in our culture at large.

The roots of neuronormativity

There are four core themes of neuronormativity:

- You must be productive, above all else.
- You must not be bothered, upset, or hurt by sensory experiences that are commonplace.
- You must speak to communicate, but you must understand and reciprocate nonverbal communication cues as well.
- You must feel emotions within a narrow window of "acceptability."

You must be productive, above all else

This particular expectation contains within it a number of sub-expectations, which are:

- Your productivity must lead to some kind of financial gain, potentially for you, but preferably for your boss.
- You must be male in order for your productivity to "count."
- Your productivity cannot inconvenience anyone with more money or power than you.

Now let's unpack all that.

Productivity that is not directly tied to a wage of some kind is not valued. A powerful example of this is stay-at-home parents, especially moms.

Stay-at-home parents are paid nothing for feeding, clothing, soothing, entertaining, and often teaching their children, something which costs thousands per month at a daycare service. And it doesn't stop at stay-at-home moms, either.

Did you know that in households with one mother and one father where both parents work full-time, the mother is still statistically more likely to do the laundry, clean the house, go grocery shopping, and prepare the meals?[2]

This leads nicely into our next point, which is that you must be male for your productivity to "count." Even though working women contribute financially to their household, they often contribute to the majority of the housework.[3]

So, moms, both stay-at-home and working, are evidence that our society does not value labor that doesn't lead to financial gain, especially if you're not a cis man.

Finally, we need to address productivity that meets all of these requirements. White men are the ones being productive, their productivity earns money, and yet our society still doesn't welcome it. Why? Because it's inconvenient for those in power.

If you need help in order to be productive, if you need assistance to communicate or lift things or read, then you are not "actually" productive. You are seen as a leech on someone else's productivity instead.

If you are able to be productive on your own, but in doing so, you disrupt or inconvenience someone who makes more money than you or has more authority than you, then that productivity doesn't count and isn't valued either.

We see this all the time in people who push back against a project that's almost finished because it won't be effective, or it isn't accessible, or it contains problematic material. Because it would be inconvenient to go back and change it, these people are nearly always ignored and then have to clean up the mess that inevitably ensues.

Neuronormativity encourages hyperindividualism, because if we see ourselves as part of something bigger, as interconnected humans, then we will no longer put up with these kinds of expectations. So instead, we are force-fed the idea that the only productivity that really counts is what we accomplish on our own.

What does all of this have to do with being AuDHD and masking?

Everything.

To talk about masking, we must talk about the dominant social expectations that we are designing our masks around. Our autism and ADHD are not solely related to ableism; they are intertwined with capitalism, racism, and every other oppressive system, because those systems shape which kinds of people are valued and which kinds are not.

And masking is all about trying to appear like one of the kinds who are valued.

You must not be bothered, hurt, or upset by sensory experiences that are commonplace

At its core, neuronormativity is all about creating this false idea of a "normal" brain, in order to other, shame, and ostracize those who do not willingly comply with the roots of neuronormativity.

And one of the easiest ways to do this is through portraying those who perceive sensory experiences differently as "too sensitive," "whiny," or even "crazy."

Or, better yet, neuronormativity might say that everyone is bothered by a certain sensory experience, but everyone else is able to cope with it, therefore it doesn't need to change, and the person complaining should just get over it too.

So, when you tell your psychiatrist that the sound of electricity in your walls really bothers you when you're trying to fall asleep, a psychiatrist unfamiliar with the high-acuity hearing common among autistic folks may try to diagnose you with psychotic symptoms, because they believe you're hearing something that doesn't exist, just because they can't hear it.

Or when you ask your friend to please chew more quietly, they may roll their eyes and make some snide remark about how you're rude, too sensitive, or trying to micromanage others.

This is just one reason AuDHDers tend to mask. At best, it is uncomfortable to share our sensory reality with others, and at worst, it's unsafe.

Did you know that up to 50 percent of people killed by the police each year are disabled?[4] It can be very literally dangerous to be unmasked.

Neuronormativity says that we should all perceive things in exactly the same way, and feel exactly the same way about those perceptions. And if you don't, your life doesn't matter to the neuronormative society around you, which results in emotional invalidation, social isolation, and/or physical danger.

You must speak to communicate, but you must also understand and utilize nonverbal communication

Trying to meet neuronormative expectations is like playing Twister with someone made of rubber. You're just a human, with bones and ligaments that limit your movement, whereas neuronormative expectations are boneless and stretchy, and you're never going to win.

One of the best examples of this is how our neuronormative society values spoken communication over any other alternative type of communication, while also demanding that we are fluent in nonverbal communication. Our society says spoken word is most important, but then if you fail to understand that a person crossing their arms means they're upset, then you're the asshole. If you don't or can't speak consistently or at all, then you're infantalized, as if your lack of speech indicates lack of any understanding.

Neuronormativity is full of these catch-22s.

You must feel emotions within a narrow window of "acceptability"

I have always had big emotions. Growing up, I was constantly called "dramatic," "too sensitive," and "crybaby." Neuronormativity would have us believe that there is a "correct" and "incorrect" way to feel about everything.

I have always been incorrect.

My reactions were never considered normal, but then, when I tried to get help for these non-normal emotions, the same people who told me I was dramatic told me I was too normal to have a mental illness.

This combination led me to believe that the problem was me. And that's exactly how neuronormativity wants you to feel.

Because shame leads to inaction. If who we are is wrong, what action could we possibly take that would be right? So we do nothing, say nothing, and eventually we start to feel like we are nothing.

And that's exactly what neuronormativity wants, to eradicate the "non-normal" brains.

Why? Because non-normal brains are the canaries in the coal mine.

We are the first ones affected by things that will eventually affect everyone. For example, capitalism has always negatively affected AuDHDers. As we saw in Chapter 4: How to Succeed at Work, around 85 percent of autistic folks are unemployed, and ADHDers often struggle with employment as well. This is largely due to the inhumane expectations that capitalism places on the workplace. Instead of working so that we can live, we are expected to live only to work.

These issues actually affect everyone; however, if you're not AuDHD, you might be more able to cope with it...for now.

But eventually capitalism will become untenable for neurotypical folks as well. We're actually starting to see this, with rising inflation and stagnating wages affecting everyone and effectively decimating the middle class. People who used to be able to live on $50,000 per year are now barely surviving.

Us AuDHDers knew about all of this first, because it affected us first. But neuronormativity says that we struggle because we are different, difficult, defective. It's not a systemic issue—it's just us. We're the problem, not the system.

If people actually paid attention to marginalized and oppressed communities, including AuDHDers, they would see these issues and might feel called to change them, either to help their fellow human beings or to keep themselves from sharing our fate.

Neuronormativity tries to eliminate the "non-normal" among us so we can't alert the others to the problem. It's much easier to accuse people who feel deeply of being "overly dramatic" or "too sensitive" than it is to actually address the problems they bring up.

Look, I'm not saying disability is purely a systemic issue or solely the result of capitalism and oppression. I am AuDHD, and even in a perfect world, that would likely come with struggles.

Here's what I am saying: maybe us "crazy" people would make more sense if we stopped looking at ourselves through a lens of "normal" or "abnormal" and started looking at ourselves through the lens of our intersecting identities, our experiences, our environment, and the overwhelming social trauma of living in a neuronormative society.

What does masking feel like?

Masking is going to look and feel different for everyone. But to me, masking is really the wrong word.

It's not about having a mask to cover up your "true" self sometimes and then taking the mask off when you want to be yourself. That's actually kind of what neurotypical contextualized behavior is like. Neurotypicals can hide their true self when they need to, but then when they're ready to be themselves, they can simply remove the mask and be themselves again.

For AuDHDers, it's more like building blocks.

When you were super young, you started to build your sense of self with your own building blocks. But your tower looked very different from others around you. People might have stared or whispered, or maybe you even had people in your life who knocked over your tower and told you to build it "right." You thought you were. You didn't understand.

But you looked around and saw how others were building their towers, and you started borrowing blocks and copying their structure until your tower looked (mostly) like everyone else's.

This metaphor more aptly captures how masking is not a "trait" of autism or ADHD, but rather a trauma response to how our world treats autistic and ADHD people. Healthy AuDHDers who are accepted from day one, who are given every accommodation they need to be successful, who live in a society that celebrates their neurotype—why would these people mask? Masking is a trauma response, not an autistic trait.

So, what does it feel like to mask? It feels scary. You feel threatened by everything around you. You always feel like you're at risk of being found out. It's often not even a conscious decision, especially for those of us who started masking very young.

Masking looks and feels different for everyone. I had several conversations with people in my community, and they provided such amazing insight into what masking is really like.

For instance, it could definitely be described as though your 2025 self is thrust back in time to the Regency era, where there are all these formal rules that everyone seems to know except for you. You have to sort of make it up as you go, try to copy the people around you, all while feeling totally out of place. Like a fraud.

You could also say that masking feels like always suppressing your natural way of doing things, even when you're doing totally ordinary, everyday things.

Some folks might describe masking as a "show" you put on so that people don't disregard you and your needs entirely.

Another excellent analogy for masking is unicycling. What if, one day, everyone started riding a unicycle everywhere instead of walking? It's obviously less convenient, but if you say that, people look at you like you're crazy. So you join them, because it's just easier than arguing and feeling wrong all the time, even though it's objectively harder for you.

Finally, I love when people compare masking to using your "customer service voice." You know, the voice you use when you work a retail job, the voice that's just a little higher, a little more chipper, a little too enthusiastic to help. But you have to use it all the time, and it's utterly exhausting.

How do I know if I'm masking?

It depends. We all mask in different ways. Because masking is dependent on the dominant social cues that surround us, it can look very different at the intersection of different identities.

An impoverished white gay man living in the south in the United States will definitely mask differently than a Black straight woman who uses a cane for her Ehler-Danlos Syndrome, and she will mask differently than a wealthy Latine nonbinary person who also has bipolar.

Here's how I finally realized I was masking, as a middle-class, white, straight, cis woman living in a predominantly white suburb the Midwest with no physical disabilities who grew up Catholic (I'm sure there are more identities I'm forgetting here, but these are the ones that have had the biggest impact on me, that I'm aware of right now):

- My husband (boyfriend at the time) pointed it out again and again. He told me that I acted completely different around my family than I did around my friends, and was another totally different person when it was just me and him.
- I ignored him because I thought everyone did that (AKA I thought it was neurotypical contextual behavior).
- I lived alone for the first time in my life and my quality of life absolutely plummeted. I sunk very deep into my obsession with my mental health, including a painful search for "who I am." I felt like my identity shifted so much that maybe I wasn't even real.
- Years later, I started to watch TikToks about autism and

ADHD. I realized that when I was completely alone, or when I felt 100% comfortable, I did a lot of that stuff.

- I slowly became more and more aware of how much I performed a version of my "self" that would make others more comfortable, even if it made me uncomfortable.
- Finally, I felt comfortable saying I was autistic and ADHD, and that I masked a lot of the time.

So it was a process. I definitely didn't know I was masking for a long time, even when others tried to tell me. Even after I learned about masking, I was pretty sure I just wasn't autistic or ADHD, and that's why I didn't show all the traits all the time.

But I know other people who have been highly aware of their masking since a relatively young age. And I know others who still aren't sure what's masking and what's not.

Some AuDHDers in my online communities say that they regret, in high school especially, how much they prioritized blending in. They learned to fly under the radar at school, but then went home and had a meltdown.

Other AuDHDers say they didn't even realize they had been masking until well into adulthood, when they burnt out from all the effort of trying to be someone they're not.

Being highly aware of your own behaviors in social situations, such as having an inner dialogue telling you to make eye contact or to move this way or that, is another way masking may show up for AuDHDers.

Your masked self is still you

Finding out that you've been masking much of your life is very disorienting and often sad. It feels like you've spent your whole life pretending, and who even are you, really?

I know it feels that way, but I want to offer you an alternative way of thinking about masking. What if your masked self is just another facet of who you are? What if your mask isn't bad or even necessarily "other" from your "true" self? What if it's all intertwined?

Here's my theory about masking and being a person.

The self is a story we are continuously telling. It evolves, it changes, the characters grow, the setting changes, and the person we were at the beginning of the story isn't a mistake or a lie; they're just not who we are at the middle or the end of the story, and maybe that's a good thing.

I mean, what would it really mean to be your "true" self anyway? Even if you were neurotypical, what would that look like? No one is consistent throughout their entire lives.

But I hear you. You're saying, "Megan, I don't have to be the exact same person every day of my life, but could I please just have a general flavor that I stick to, that feels good for me, instead of swinging from one flavor to the next, or constantly being a flavor I don't even like?"

Yeah, I get that.

If you want to unmask, if that will make you feel more authentic, I understand that. Many of us feel that way.

How to unmask

Unmasking is often a lifelong process. It's not something you can tackle in a weekend or in a few therapy sessions or by reading this book. Unmasking is about being yourself in a world that doesn't support you. It's about discovering yourself in a world that has done everything it can to hide you away from the world, and from yourself.

Honestly, for me, I'd spent so long acting neurotypical that in order to even figure out what my natural neurodivergent tendencies were, I had to "act" neurodivergent.

This looked like trying out more obvious stims, like hand flapping or spinning, dopamine dressing in bright, comfy clothes, not white-knuckling my way through a verbal shutdown, and instead simply allowing myself to stop talking.

All of this was…awkward.

It didn't feel natural at first, not at all. Which, of course, made me feel totally lost. I knew I wasn't neurotypical, and acting like I was felt draining and false, but here I was trying to act autistic or act ADHD, and that felt false too! Literally, what the hell?

So, here's what I wish I had known back then.

Unmasking advice from the community

Since unmasking looks so different for all of us, I didn't want to solely give my own perspective on how to unmask. I talked with my online community, and many of them said things like "If you figure it out, be sure to let me know, because I have no idea."

But lots of them had great advice, so here it is:

- Some AuDHDers unmask by keeping track of the times they have managed to be themselves and how good it felt. It's like evidence that being yourself is safe. Remember, it's okay to unmask slowly so that you (and others around you) can adapt.
- Other AuDHDers go cold turkey and try to behave however feels "natural" for a few weeks, just to see what happens.
- The best part of unmasking is being able to embrace your weirdness, recognizing that you're different, and that that's a good thing. Though it's also important to admit that unmasking can be exhausting. Prepare to spend a lot more time resting.

- If you find yourself struggling with unmasking, it can be very helpful to talk with a trusted person about why unmasking matters and how you want to experiment with it.

Personally, here are some questions I would ask myself if I could go back and start the unmasking process all over again:

- Who would I want to be if I knew that person would be accepted and loved and celebrated?
- How would I act if I were interacting with myself? What would feel most natural?
- Who are the people in my life who might be open to seeing new sides of me?
- Who are the people in my life that are unsafe, unsupportive, and/or unwilling to try to understand me beyond the version of me in their heads?
- If my discomfort and distress mattered just as much as everyone else's, if I could trust the people around me to actually *want* to support me in times of distress, how would my behavior reflect my distress?

I think these questions really show how difficult it can be to unmask. It's not about putting a mask on and then taking it off. Masking is built into our very being. If we want to unmask, we need to tear ourselves down and rebuild.

And there are lots of reasons people don't want to, or can't, do that.

Is masking a "privilege"?

Yes. And no. It's complicated.

If you are a highly masked individual, you know that masking does not feel like a privilege. It's a nightmare. You're a jester in front of a royal court who make fun of you, even when you try to perform for them. You can't imagine what hell life would be if you stopped performing.

And that's why some people who cannot mask consider it a privilege to be able to do so. It is indeed hellish to go through life unable to hide the things about yourself that society collectively hates. It is deeply traumatic to be seen for who you are against your will, to want to hide, to want to blend in and be completely unable to.

I think it's important to remember that "privilege" doesn't mean "easy peasy life with no struggles." It means having an advantage that makes life easier or lacking a disadvantage that makes life harder.

Masking is sort of a double-edged sword. It affords us opportunity to control the narrative around who we are, which can give us opportunities we might miss out on without our mask. However, the psychoemotional toll (and sometimes the resulting physical toll) it takes on us cannot be ignored. Living life unmasked, if accompanied by social support, can be wildly freeing. However, without that social support, it can be deeply isolating, or even dangerous.

At the end of the day, your unmasking journey is your own, and it is only one part of your story as an AuDHDer. Unmasking isn't the be-all and end-all of self-acceptance and self-love. You don't have to be a purely authentic raw nerve to be a "good" AuDHDer. But you also don't have to hide your neurodivergent traits from yourself in order to tolerate who you are.

You are good. Your unmasked self is good, and your masked self is good, and the part of you that is seeking connection with yourself and with others is so, so good too.

EXERCISES

➔ Write down three ways you would behave differently if you were confident you were safe to do so. Here are some examples for inspiration, but feel free to come up with your own:
  - Stim freely
  - Avoid eye contact or make intense eye contact, whatever feels right
  - Tell people when you're uncomfortable
  - Create a meltdown plan so you can experience distress safely
  - Invest in comfy clothes and wear them on repeat
  - Ask clarifying questions when you're confused
  - Say goodbye to friends who make you feel small for being yourself

➔ List the ways you can increase your self-acceptance even when you can't unmask. Here are some examples for inspiration, but feel free to come up with your own:
  - Have a masking plan/routine so that it requires less cognitive energy
  - Embrace your mask as just another aspect of yourself, rather than a "false" self
  - Take frequent trips to the bathroom, for a walk around the office, or even outside so that you can take a quick break from masking
  - Have safe unmasking spaces outside of the spaces where you need to be masked
  - Remember that keeping yourself safe is just as important as being yourself, and you are not bad for masking

KEY TAKEAWAY

→ Unmasking is not a magic bullet that will solve all your AuDHD struggles, and it isn't possible for everyone in every situation. But learning to be ourselves when and how we can is essential to our wellbeing.

Part 3
Healing with AuDHD

CHAPTER 7

Disability Is Not a Dirty Word

Okay, let's start this chapter by being totally honest.

Just a few years ago, I would have absolutely balked at this chapter title. I would have been confused, and intimidated, and maybe even a little offended.

Because for a long time, I really did believe that "disability" was a dirty word. Maybe not an insult, but definitely taboo. I felt like it was okay to "make your peace" with being disabled, but it wasn't something to celebrate.

And some folks still feel this way, and that's okay.

There's no one way to think about disability and AuDHD. Over the years, I've held many different perspectives on this, but all of them have been very black-and-white. And now, pretty recently in fact, I've started developing a gray-er point of view, one that focuses more on being inclusive than on being "right."

So, as we enter this chapter, I encourage you to give it a chance, to read with a critical eye, and to take what works for you and ditch the rest.

And please, seek out others' perspectives on this as well. Mine is just one story. And there is no single story of AuDHD.

What is disability?

I actually stared at a blank page for over an hour while writing this section of the book, trying to figure out where to even start. There are so many ways to define disability, and it felt wrong to choose just one angle.

So, let's explore how the three main definitions of disability intersect with AuDHD:

- legal
- medical
- lived experience.

Legal definition of disability

There are countless legal definitions of disability, since every country, territory, province, and more have their own legal bodies. Since I live in the United States, I'll go ahead and provide the legal definition of a person with a disability as defined by our Americans with Disabilities Act (ADA):

- Has a physical or mental impairment that substantially limits one or more major life activities, or
- Has a history or *record* of an impairment (such as cancer that is in remission), or
- Is *regarded* as having such an impairment by others even if the individual does not actually have a disability (such as a person who has scars from a severe burn that does not limit any major life activity).[1]

The first thing to note here is the word "or" included in each bullet point. You do no need to have all three of these requirements in order to be disabled. Rather, you only need one.

I know many AuDHDers don't see their neurodivergence as fitting this definition at all, as many of us don't consider our AuDHD a "mental impairment," and many of us mask so well that others don't perceive us as having any "mental impairment" either.

That being said, many of us do agree that we experience limitations in our daily life due to our autism and/or ADHD. If that resonates with you more than the wording provided by the ADA, let's look at the medical definition of disability.

Medical definition of disability

According to the International Classification of Functioning, Disability and Health (ICF), which is the framework used by the World Health Organization (WHO), disability has three dimensions:

- activity (and activity restrictions)
- participation (and participation restrictions)
- body structure and function (and impairment thereof).[2]

Here, we can see how AuDHD might fit a little better. Nearly every AuDHDer has limitations on what kinds of activities we can do, and how we can participate in them. For example, I cannot fill out paperwork. I want to be able to do it, I feel like I should be able to do it, but at the end of the day, I just can't. It's a combination of my ADHD difficulty with details and my autistic need for very explicit instructions that most forms lack.

Another common example is driving. Many AuDHDers can drive, and many cannot. Driving is a very social activity, which means our autistic struggles often show up on the road as well. We may struggle to merge because we can't get a read on other drivers to anticipate what they're going to do, and we might follow speed limits to the letter and end up getting tailgated by frustrated drivers who take speed limits more as a suggestion than an actual limit.

ADHD can also impact our ability to drive, so much so that studies show that ADHDers are statistically more likely to get into car accidents than non-ADHDers, likely due to our distractibility.[3]

When you combine our ADHD distractibility and our autistic difficulty understanding the intentions of other drivers, driving can become exceptionally difficult for many AuDHDers.

It might feel a bit odd to say that as AuDHDers, we have "body structure and function" impairments, but when you consider the brain to be part of the body, it's pretty clear that our brains have function differences (and maybe structural differences as well, though the research is catching up on that!).

Finally, let's look at a lived experience definition of disability, based not on lawsuits or differential diagnostics, but on what it's like to be disabled.

Lived experience definition of disability

When I first started writing this chapter, I fully anticipated writing it solely from my perspective, with the help of considerable research.

But when I went to define disability, I saw how lacking the legal and medical definitions were, and realized we definitely needed a lived experience definition as well. And for me to provide a lived experience definition of disability, I knew I needed to talk to the AuDHD community. I needed more perspectives.

I reached out to my community on Instagram and on my email list, and asked a few key questions:

- Do you identify as disabled?
- Why do you identify as disabled, or why do you not? If it's complicated, feel free to infodump on that here.

- If you *do* identify as disabled, how would you define disability through a lived experience lens? "It's Complicated" folks are welcome to provide their definition as well. (If you don't identify as disabled, no worries! Just put N/A for "not applicable" in this slot.)

I received over 100 answers, and they taught me so much about how varied our community is on this topic, and how we can all identify differently for different reasons and still be AuDHD together.

So, let's explore why some AuDHDers don't identify as disabled and why others do, and then after that, we'll explore how the AuDHDers who *do* identify as disabled would define disability.

"I am not disabled because..."

Out of all the responses, 10 percent said they would not consider themselves disabled and 42 percent said, "It's Complicated." Among those two categories, a few key themes emerged.

First, many folks said they didn't feel that their ADHD or autism negatively impacted their life, and therefore they were not disabled. Here are a few excerpts that will help expand on this point:

> "...even though I have some health issues on both the physical and mental spectrum I find myself lucky to be able to do everyday activities without those problems interfering that much with how I get around and I do have the ability to be open socially and with new activities because I don't have anything that stops me from that. I appreciate that aspect of my life..."
>
> AS

> "...I've never seen myself as disabled, just mental health issues."
>
> SARAH B.

" I feel impeded—I can do my job fine but I'd have been able to do it much better as a non divergent."

BARB

" For me, being disabled means that something is missing, inside of me or outside of me (=a body part) or that I can't use a part of my body. I don't identify as disabled, because I'm not missing any part of my body, I can use all parts of my body, my brain is working properly (just with ADHD)."

ANNIKA H.

Second, several respondents said that they don't identify as disabled because they feel that society doesn't see them as disabled, though they acknowledge they do struggle with daily functioning in many ways. Here are a few excerpts that will give you a better picture of this point of view:

" It took me a very long time to even accept the term, and I don't use it around my family because of the negative stigma attached to the word."

TIANNA S.

" ...since I spent much of my life around disabled people, I have a weird belief that I don't have the right to consider myself disabled. (They've all been worse off than me, my brain tells me. My brain also tells me to shape up...)"

LINDA D.

" I grew up in a time where anyone who was disabled was *visibly* disabled. No one talked about invisible disability. I know that my brain is different, and that it causes me to act in ways that confuse others. Since I grew up and learned to mask at an early

153

age, it's hard to think of myself as disabled, although my life is impacted daily by some of my brain's tendencies."

ANONYMOUS

" ...society have conditioned me to think you are just lazy if you don't have a physical disability..."

RICKI G.

" ...People just don't believe you're disabled if you're working full time and taking care of a family member. They don't see the cost, just the actions. It's a lot of 'but you don't *look* sick.' Yeah Brenda? Try living in my body for five minutes."

SHERRY S.

" ...I think I'm able to not identify as disabled because I live a very fortunate and privileged life, where I don't need to identify as disabled to get the accommodations that I ask for... But if I really think about whether there are things that some people can do that I cannot because of my mental health and neurodivergence, the answer is yes, and isn't that really the definition of disability?"

ELIZABETH K.

Third, several people said they aren't disabled because they view neurotypical society as the problem. In an accommodating environment, they are not disabled, and therefore they don't feel comfortable assuming that label because it makes them the "problem" when, in reality, our ableist society is the problem. Here are a few quotes to better describe this:

" I feel that if I am disabled, it's by the neurotypical world rather than by my autism. When I'm in my own environment, with my neurodivergent friends, I don't have issues with communication or the like. It's the outside world that is the problem—other people's expectations of how I should behave, loud and bright shops etc."

RACHAEL L.

" ...I went 40 years without considering myself disabled and very little has changed other than my knowledge. So accepting the label 'disabled' is difficult. For me, this is just my life. The reframing is a journey that I'm still on. I've also realized the label of disabled is more about others' perception of me than my own understanding. I have been understanding and accommodating myself my whole life. Explaining it to others is where that label helps most..."

ANGIE L.

" I don't have an official adhd diagnosis... So, I don't identify as disabled and other than with my sister and closest friends, I don't talk about the very real possibility that I am adhd..."

ANONYMOUS

Finally, many of the people who said "It's Complicated" in response to the question "Do you identify as disabled?" said that they felt they couldn't claim the identity of "disabled" because they didn't have a professional, on-paper diagnosis, or that they didn't see the point of identifying as disabled because it wouldn't provide any support where they live. Here's how they describe it in their own words:

" It's complicated because I'm 99.9% sure I'm autistic and I'm in the process of getting a diagnosis but nothing happening for me... I just don't have a diagnosis and that's the only reason I can't confidently say I'm disabled."

ZAHRA Q.

> "...I don't think identifying as disabled would make any difference, as I don't think ADHD is recognized as a disability where I live (Ontario, Canada). At least not in terms of getting support. My employer would not make any accommodations if I identified as disabled with ADHD, so there isn't much point. However, I do think ADHD is disabling in many ways..."
>
> ANONYMOUS

> "It feels strange to identify as disabled because I am ADHD and only self-diagnosed autistic. In Germany, ADHD is not really considered as a disability so it feels strange to use that term. But I still feel my surroundings disabling me, so I want to be able to proudly say that I am disabled. It would also make it easier to 'justify' my struggles."
>
> MEL

"I am disabled because..."

On the other hand, 49 percent of respondents said they are disabled, and once again, some key themes emerged when I looked at the answers.

First, lots of people said they identify as disabled because they have a diagnosis that is literally categorized as a disability (like both autism and ADHD) and so therefore they are disabled. Here's how they describe this in their own words:

> "I identify as an autistic person, and autism is classified as a disability, therefore I am considered disabled..."
>
> MICHELLE K.

> "I identify as disabled [because] I inhabit multiple developmental, mental health, and physical disabilities. While all of these may be invisible, I still live in a society that perpetuates systems of

oppression and exclusion that impact my ability to comfortably move through life."

XERO X.

Second, many respondents who said they do identify as disabled said it's because they have very real limitations in their daily life. Each person has their own way of explaining this, and here are a few excerpts to give you a clearer picture of this point of view:

> "I identify as disabled because my neurodivergence has hindered a lot of my life growing up and even more so now as an adult."

KELLIE P.

> "...The way my communication and organization skills have regressed, my memory has worsened, my body aches 24/7, I'm constantly fatigued...all of these things brought about from long-term masking and the trauma of living an ill-fitting life, they lead me to use the use term."

STELLEN K.

> "I have both autism and ADHD. I do identify as disabled because both conditions do present challenges for me in terms of executive functioning, maintaining relationships, over or understimuation, and difficulty identifying emotions among other challenges."

KJ D.

> "...My ADHD still limits and challenges me every day, and it is a constant battle. I can manage some of it with coping skills, resources, and accommodations, but that does not remove the barriers and challenges that come with my disability. The way my brain functions causes me to struggle in so many ways, which is why I have a disability."

KRYSTYNA K.

Third, lots of people said they identify as disabled because even if they don't have a ton of hard and fast limitations, doing "normal" things takes them a lot more time and effort than it does for people who are not AuDHD. Here are some excerpts that describe this point of view:

> I feel disabled because of the amount of work I have to put in just be a seemingly functional person... People around me always see me so happy and hardworking but don't see all the time and energy that went into just showing up here today."
>
> AGUSTIN T.

> Disabled for me means struggling in daily tasks and feeling easily overwhelmed by 'few tasks' in a day. I've always had to do 10X more efforts to just be in the norm and keep going with kids of my age, and seeing that my efforts weren't very noticeable by my parents or teachers, I felt not enough."
>
> SALMA R.

> I do identify as disabled...being disabled is not bad, and I definitely am privileged in my experience as I can camouflage into society, however I do experience major struggles that my peers don't have. While people love to admire and congratulate my many achievements, and I am proud of all of them, I often struggle with feeding myself in regular intervals, hygiene routines, and I also can spiral super fast into a dissociative state from guilt or shame..."
>
> SIRI N.

> ...I am always exhausted when others aren't. I am too tired and too much in pain for a lot of things including sports, work and meeting friends..."
>
> ANYA J.

Finally, some folks consider themselves disabled because their differences, struggles, and/or limitations cannot be removed from who they are as a person. Here's how they describe this in their own words:

> I have multiple disabilities including physical, psychological and developmental that make things difficult from day to day. No amount of accommodation will make me fully functional."
>
> SARAH S.

> The current world and culture I'm living in is too loud, too bright, too busy, too social, too disorganized, fast, unkind, intolerant for my neurotype. I'm exhausted and in pain almost always. It's getting harder and harder to have enough energy and strength to survive. I am unable. It's likely to kill me sooner than a more abled person."
>
> LOUISE G.

Lived experience definition of disability, in the words of disabled folks

As you can tell from the experiences shared, disability is different for everyone. And it's so much more than just a legal or medical experience. It's social, it's personal, and it depends hugely on what it's like to live with your disability. Here's what some respondents had to say about what disability is to them:

> Disability in the sense of mental (and in some ways physically as well) is the inability to perform daily tasks the way neurotypicals do, because our bucket of woe is much smaller and sits on a flimsy shelf instead of the big ass desk that the big ass buckets of woe the neurotypicals get. Meaning when little things happen like the construction outside may be super bothersome to

some folks, making them unable to focus or really feel comfortable at all, to others it's mildly distracting, and to neurotypicals they might not even notice it let alone it barely disrupts their day; those types of things add to the bucket of woe for the disabled…"

ELIZABETH K.

"I can do somethings other people cannot (I'm gifted, very out-of-the-box problem solving but don't like that word as I'm not academic or functional as an employee) but basic daily necessities are hard. Like self-care, food, shopping (I have a problem in supermarkets), and school was very stressful. I'm a mum and struggle sometimes with noise, fatigue, and overwhelm… People misunderstand me as I can create and present a two-hour-long workshop but not endure 15 minutes waiting in a queue."

HEATHER L.

"…I spent so long being in denial of my disability because 'it doesn't stop me from doing things that I want to do.' But that's because I didn't have room to stop, so I was burning myself out. While I still have days where I'm frustrated, I now look at my disability as something that will make it more difficult for me to do things I want to do, and that's okay. I need to take the time to make sure I'm not exhausted or burnt out before continuing, and that's completely fine. I just need everyone else to be as patient with me as I am with myself."

LAYNE S.

"I would define disability as something that blocks you from carrying out the activities most people carry out with ease. Certain activities can take more time and effort, or can leave negative consequences such as being exhausted afterwards. For me, I go to college, I get through my days with little support and appear to be functioning 'normally,' but when I get home I'm wiped out, I need at least an hour before I can do anything else, I really struggle with getting homework done because I don't have the energy, and I don't have the capacity to do much else for the rest of the day... People may discount autism and ADHD as disabilities because 'it's all in the head' and there isn't a clear physical limitation, but no matter how much I want to do something and push myself, I often can't. Society isn't built for neurodivergent brains so we can't function as others do, no matter how hard we try."

ANONYMOUS

" Our society has expectations of a 'normal' way of being either in body or mind and when you cannot conform to that expectation for whatever reason, or it costs you greatly in mental or physical health, then you are 'disabled' or 'differently abled' than the expected."

LARISSA R.

" ...I think disability really is defined by not easily accessing the things society has made accessible to the neurotypical, wealthy, white, cis, male members of western society. But it's on purpose. If we held a viewpoint that everyone has value and we created a world where everyone had the opportunity to engage in a way that worked for them, would there even be disability?"

ANONYMOUS

" I think of it as extra challenges that require my attention, time, money, treatments, etc. that other people don't seem to have. So they have more energy, time, mental capacity and resources to just do life..."

WILL L.

So...what does this mean for me?

It means whatever you want it to mean.

No, seriously. I hope this chapter doesn't make you feel like you "should" identify as disabled or "shouldn't," but rather helps you look at AuDHD through a lens that considers the possibility of disability as neutral instead of "bad."

The question is, how do we do that?

And hey, why is that so hard?

Ableism, my friend. Lots of ableism.

What is ableism?

Ableism, like lots of other -isms in our society, is baked in. It's not a flaw in the system—it's part of the system, designed to uphold patterns of oppression. And it interacts with all the other -isms too, creating intersectional problems for disabled people of color, multiply disabled folks, disabled trans and gender nonconforming folks, and so much more.

Ableism, put plainly, is the harmful belief that it is best to be non-disabled, and that disability makes a person "less than" in some way compared to a non-disabled person.

At first glance, for many of you, this might not feel like a huge problem. I know that's how I felt at first when I learned about ableism.

Like...of course we should accept people as they are, but...isn't it preferable *not* to have a disability? Especially with all the definitions given above, even the lived experience ones, emphasizing limitations, struggle, and pain?

Yes...and no.

Yes, of course we want to limit people's suffering in this

lifetime, but no, the way to do that is not to somehow eradicate disability. That often leads to something called eugenics.

Eugenics is another complex topic, but at its core, it's the idea that some people are more worthy of passing on their genes to the next generation than others.

Yeah, just reading that, you can probably tell there's some white supremacy nonsense happening there. And you're right. But there's also rampant ableism.

If the goal is for no one to be disabled anymore, then are people born with disabilities morally (or, heaven forbid, legally) obligated to not have children? And in a post-Roe world, what does that mean for disabled folks in the United States who can get pregnant?

There is a long and disturbing global history of forced sterilization of Black folks, disabled folks, and more, and it's not all behind us. In 2020, an official whistleblower complaint was filed, saying that the Immigrations and Customs Enforcement (ICE) was forcibly sterilizing detainees in the United States at the Mexico-US border.[4]

So eugenics rhetoric isn't just dangerous in principle. It has very real, tangible consequences for oppressed groups who are often seen as less worthy of passing on their genes and creating more people like them in some way.

Now you might be thinking, "Megan, I never said disabled folks can't have kids! I just meant, isn't it better to be able to do everything? Isn't disability inherently...harder? What's so wrong with wanting people to have an easier life?"

The thing is, disability is part of the natural diversity of humanity. And the only way to get rid of it (or even reduce it significantly) is eugenics and/or the extermination of disabled folks.

Even though some folks would gladly accept a cure for their disability (including many AuDHDers), it should always be *their* choice, not the result of societal pressure saying that the way they are is wrong, or that there's not room for them in society.

So, if the goal is not to get rid of disability, what should the goal be?

Disability acceptance, regardless of abilities

Do you use glasses or contacts? If so, you are disabled, by every definition provided above.

But in our society, we rarely think of nearsightedness as a disability. That's because it's so easily accommodated. But it's more than that.

What makes nearsightedness such an interesting example of disability acceptance is not just that it's so easily accommodated; it's that our society offers little to no shame about being nearsighted or needing glasses.

Our accommodations are seen as very reasonable, and no one gets stares or whispers following them when they go out while wearing glasses. No one assumes we are not competent. We're not seen as "abusing the system" to gain an "unfair advantage."

We just need glasses. No big deal.

So, why are so many other disabilities so much more stigmatized? I think this is because glasses, contacts, or even Lasik can make it so your disability is functionally nonexistent.

It's the perfect disability: one that can be accommodated to the point that the disability no longer impacts daily living, and inconveniences no one except maybe the disabled person (paying for glasses, having to put in contacts every morning, etc.).

But what about disabilities where this isn't possible? What about disabilities that can only be accommodated somewhat, or disabilities that more prominently affect those around us?

This is where our society has a long way to go. Because the goal isn't just to accept and embrace disability when it can be accommodated enough for people to live a "normal" life.

It's to accept and embrace disability however it presents. No matter how obvious, inconvenient, or impairing.

Our goal as a society should not be to optimize every individual to some standard of "perfection," but rather to create a society where all kinds of people can live and thrive and struggle and just...be. Regardless of our abilities.

Ableism and AuDHD

So where does AuDHD come in here?

Autism and ADHD belong to a category of disabilities that are often called "invisible disabilities" because there are no physical disabilities inherent in AuDHD (though there are many associations with physical disabilities, like Ehlers-Danlos Syndrome (EDS), Postural Orthostatic Tachycardia Syndrome (POTS) and more).

But I prefer the term introduced by Sonny Jane Wise: ignored disabilities.[5]

Wise says that although the term "invisible disabilities" has brought increased awareness to the wide variety of disabilities out there, they prefer the term "ignored disabilities" because, in their words, "Our disabilities are not hidden or invisible. Our disabilities are misunderstood, denied and ignored by society."

All of this makes me think of one of the sections under the "I am not disabled because..." heading: where people said they don't identify as disabled, not because they're not, but because society doesn't acknowledge their disability.

It also makes me think of the section under the "I am disabled because..." heading: where people said they don't necessarily have the limitations most people think of when they think of disability, but they have to work so much harder to be "normal" than other people.

Basically, I can see how many of us AuDHDers would consider our autism and ADHD to be ignored disabilities, whether we personally consider ourselves disabled or not.

I mean, people definitely notice that I'm late all the time and forget everything. People have no problem calling me "melodramatic" or "too sensitive." People know I'm different.

It's just when I try to assert my identity as a disabled person that they suddenly pretend they don't see all the signs.

As Wise says, "they associate these things with personal failings or flaws rather than a part of our disability."

Autism and ADHD are very commonly seen as personal failings. Our sensory sensitivities are exaggerations, our social communication differences are rude, our forgetfulness is carelessness, and our emotional sensitivity is manipulative.

But what if none of that is true? How would our self-esteem shift if society saw our abilities, however limited they might be, as enough?

All disabled folks deserve to exist, and to be accepted and celebrated for who we are. Whether you're physically disabled, intellectually disabled, developmentally disabled, or otherwise disabled, you are good. You are enough.

Our society says otherwise, but society has been wrong many times before, and it is wrong about you now. AuDHD is a disability to some, not a disability to others, but regardless, I want you to know how incredibly needed you are in this world.

It doesn't matter if you can't work a full-time job or if you can't date or if you can't fill out paperwork or if you can't speak.

Your value in this lifetime goes so far beyond neurotypical expectations of success.

Internalized ableism: The neuronormativity is calling from inside the house

We are participants in this world, and as a result, we absorb everything that's out there.

Including ableism.

Being AuDHD doesn't mean you magically don't absorb ableism. In fact, because you're more likely to have ableist remarks and attitudes thrown at you, you might end up absorbing it even more than someone who's neurotypical.

Some AuDHDers grow up hearing things like "ADHD isn't an excuse to be lazy" or "Just because you're autistic doesn't mean you can be rude" and they know it's not okay. They reject ableism like a bad organ transplant, and often this makes them even more of a target. They may get even more ableist remarks, like "Don't make me the bad guy when you're the one messing up."

Other AuDHDers, like me, have a hard time realizing that other people can be wrong. I know I didn't really realize people could lie or that they might present their opinions like facts for a long time, so I just...believed everybody.

When people told me I was flakey, I was like, "Yeah, sounds right, can't argue with that."

That's the other thing: AuDHD does come with very real struggles and limitations. So when someone criticizes the way we do something, we can't really argue because we *do* do that, y'know?

At least, that's what I thought for a long time. And that's how we get internalized ableism.

Internalized ableism is when we absorb all the negative messages about being different and/or disabled, we believe them, and we start directing ableism toward ourselves.

It's our way of beating people to the punch. If we beat ourselves up for being disorganized and messy, other people won't feel the need to say something too, because we already said, "Oh, sorry for all the mess, I'm an absolute pig, I know."

We accept others' ableist comments, we assume the blame for our struggles, rather than understanding them within a context of disability, and worst of all?

Sometimes we dish it back out.

Lateral ableism as a form of masking

Want to know one of the quickest shortcuts to making people believe you're neurotypical?

Pick on the neurodivergent kids.

It sucks, and it's not okay, but please remember that masking is a survival strategy, not something we do for fun or because we like it. And for many AuDHDers, this included being dismissive, rude, or even actively harmful to people who were just like us, but couldn't hide it as well.

I remember doing this less with the other kids at school, and more with fictional characters. Laughing at the sensitive characters on TV and calling them silly felt like a way to connect with the people in my life who thought I was too sensitive. Maybe if I made fun of this trait too, I could earn love in ways that I couldn't by just being my sensitive self.

Lateral ableism can also look like judging people with disabilities different from yours. Like, it's okay to be AuDHD, but schizophrenia? No way, that's "crazy."

This is lateral ableism. All disabilities are different, but they're all good and okay. They should all be accepted and understood. Making ourselves feel better about *our* disability by making it seem better than a different disability is crab behavior.

If you put a bunch of crabs in a tall bucket of water, they are totally capable of escape. However, what usually happens is the crabs pull each other down, in an attempt to use the other crabs to get out.

We get farther by working together. Rising tides lift all boats. Why drag each other down when we could all get out and start pinching the people who put us in the bucket in the first place.

KEY TAKEAWAY

→ Some AuDHDers consider themselves to be disabled, while others do not. Regardless, disability is not a bad thing, and it's vital for all AuDHDers to respect each other's point of view on disability.

EXERCISES

→ How does the word "disabled" make you feel? Do you consider yourself disabled? Take the time to journal (or pace and talk to yourself, if you're a verbal processor, like me) on what this word means, and whether or not it applies to you.

→ How have you internalized ableism from people, media, and society around you? Identify one way you can challenge that ableism. For example, let's say you notice that you have the internalized belief that therapy is for weak-minded people. Maybe you could journal on ten reasons going to therapy actually exemplifies mental strength, or even try going to therapy once yourself.

> → Go out of your way to follow someone who speaks to the lived experience of a disability that's totally different from AuDHD. Identify similarities between your experiences, but also identify differences. And if you love their content, DM them and let them know!!!

Inner Child Work for AuDHDers

How to Heal the Wound of Being Different

Do you ever wish you could go back in time? Maybe tell yourself everything you know now about autism and ADHD, or shake certain adults in your life and tell them to be more understanding?

Yeah, don't we all.

Unfortunately, none of us can rewrite history. But believe it or not, it is possible to go back in time, in a way.

The younger version of you still exists as part of who you are now. In fact, who you are now is a collection of lots of past selves, from childhood to the teenage years and beyond.

As we grow up, we don't cease to be our old selves; we just change, and we carry all the previous versions of ourselves within us.

This might sound weird, but I promise it's true.

I know, because I've done a lot of inner child work. This is a practice where you get in touch with those past selves, listen to what they need, and do what you can to provide it to them, here and now.

Sure, in some ways, it's too late. The damage done in our child-hoods can last a lifetime, and there's no way to literally change our past experiences.

But that doesn't mean we're doomed to be in pain forever. Inner child work doesn't rewrite the past, but it can help us write a better future.

What is inner child work? Do I really need it?

I know this chapter might sound a little out there, a little strange, maybe even kind of fake to you right now, and hey, if inner child work isn't right for you, that's always okay. But my job is to introduce you to as many healing modalities and coping strategies as I can, and to be honest, nothing has been as healing for me as inner child work has been.

So, what is it?

Inner child work can take many forms, but here's the gist: you want to engage in some kind of practice that allows you to get in touch with who you used to be when you were little. How you felt, how you saw the world, what you thought, all of it.

Then you want to listen. What is your inner child trying to say? To you, to your parents, to your childhood friends, to themselves, what do they want to say?

Once you've listened, you can talk. Tell your inner child what they needed to hear back in the day, but no one was capable of telling them at the time.

You can be the adult you always needed.

And yeah, like I said, this won't rewrite the past, but it can be incredibly healing for your inner child to hear that you love them. That you're proud of them. That you understand them. I mean...just picture that for a minute. Imagine ten-year-old you hearing from a trusted adult that they are good enough. How would that feel?

Honestly, I think everyone in the world needs some inner child work, but it's been especially important for me as an AuDHDer because being AuDHD (especially going unrecognized for so long) often leads to complex, developmental, and/or attachment trauma.

Why does this happen?

Well, it can happen for a lot of reasons.

Bullying

Many AuDHDers experience serious bullying in school. Maybe not in a "Haha, you're autistic" kind of way (though many early diagnosed folks absolutely did experience that type of bullying) but in a "Haha, I find all of your autistic traits weird and off-putting even though I don't have a name for why you're like that" kind of way. Some AuDHDers even experienced bullying from teachers and staff at their school, often in a "I need to make this kid a scapegoat so none of the other kids think it's okay to act like this" kind of way, or in a "If I encourage the kids to tease them, the social pressure will encourage them to act more normal which will benefit them in the long run" kind of way.

Regardless of what kind of bullying you experienced, I just want you to know that bullying can absolutely be traumatic (go back to Chapter 2 where we explore what trauma is and why it includes so much more than just near-death experiences). What you went through sucked and it should never have happened, and it's okay if it didn't make you stronger. It's okay if it just made you mad and scared.

Childhood emotional neglect

Do you ever get the feeling that something was deeply wrong with your childhood, but when you look back, everything is like... totally fine? You were always taken care of, had food and a house and maybe your parents were happily married, maybe you were able to participate in sports and clubs, go bike riding through your suburban neighborhood, and you just can't explain why you feel so traumatized.

For many AuDHDers, the answer is something called childhood emotional neglect.

This is where you had most or all your physical needs met, and you didn't experience the presence of anything bad, like abuse, but you had a notable lack of emotional support.

This is especially common for AuDHDers because we often have very different emotional needs than neurotypical kids. We have meltdowns, and sensitivities, and don't often communicate with our caregivers in ways they might expect.

We need different things than a neurotypical child might need. And when those needs are treated like "preferences" or we're told we're "just being picky" or maybe we're accommodated but we're made to feel like a burden each and every time, that is a direct invalidation of our very real, actual needs. It's emotional neglect.

Plus, it's worth noting that both autism and ADHD are highly genetic, and our parents may have experienced childhood emotional neglect as well in response to their own neurodivergence and see it as the norm, and go on to treat us the same way.

Childhood emotional neglect might sound like less of a big deal than things like bullying or abuse, but here's the truth: when you learn from a young age that your very being is incorrect and not welcome with the people who are supposed to love you the most, you learn all kinds of additional messages, like "Love is conditional and I have to be good enough in order to earn it," or "People are inherently unsafe because no one can give me what I need," or "I am a needy, whiny, bad person who asks way too much."

It sucks. And it shouldn't have happened to you. It didn't make you tough—it made you hurt. And it's okay to tend to those wounds now.

A daisy in a rose garden

Okay, what if the word "neglect" sounds way too extreme for your situation? What if you *know* your caregivers did their best, and so did you, and you both love each other so much, and it just… didn't fit?

This is one of the cruel realities of our world, that sometimes parents have a child they love more than anything, but never fully understand. And it's not your fault or their fault—it just is.

And when neurotypical parents have an AuDHD child, this can happen so easily.

You're like a daisy in a rose garden. Roses and daisies are both beautiful, but they have very different needs when it comes to soil and water and sunlight.

Just like that, you might have very different needs when it comes to emotions and your sensory environment and friends, compared to the rest of your family.

And that led to some miscommunications and probably some hurt feelings and maybe even trauma, even though no one wanted to traumatize you.

The good news is that daisies can come to appreciate roses and vice versa. Acknowledging this mismatch and recognizing the hard work you're both doing to connect with each other can lead to a beautiful relationship.

How to do inner child work

Okay, it's important to do inner child work to heal this stuff, but how? What are the practical steps to inner child work?

Well, everyone does inner child work a little differently and you should feel free to explore a variety of strategies. Here are some of the most common methods:

- EMDR (eye-movement desensitization and reprocessing)
- EFT (emotional freedom techniques)
- journaling.

Not sure what EMDR or EFT are exactly? No worries, we'll explore them more in the coming sections. For now, just know this: inner child work can be intense. While you are absolutely the expert on yourself and should feel free to do this work alone if you so choose, I would just like to say that it can be very beneficial to have the assistance of a therapist or coach when delving deep into some of these things.

EMDR

Eye-movement desensitization and reprocessing, or EMDR, is a specific type of therapy commonly used in trauma healing. It relies on something called bilateral stimulation, which sounds fancy, but is honestly just providing some kind of sensory input on both the left and right sides of your body somehow. Some common ways people do this include:

- a light bar which shows a light moving back and forth
- crossing your arms over your chest and tapping your shoulders
- holding small handheld devices that vibrate slightly back and forth.

Heck, studies have even found that Tetris can provide bilateral stimulation, and people with PTSD who play Tetris for 60 minutes per day (in addition to traditional EMDR therapy) showed better outcomes than those who only did the EMDR.[1]

But it's not just bilateral stimulation that makes EMDR so effective. It's the desensitization and reprocessing bit as well. Some EMDR therapists use this therapeutic tool to go back to the traumatic event in the client's mind and re-experience it, but this time, with an anchor to safety through the bilateral stimulation and the presence of the therapist.

If that sounds like it would be entirely too overwhelming, and like it would trigger you more than it's worth, you're not alone. Many EMDR therapists do not have the client relive the traumatic experience. Rather, they have the client get in touch with some of the feelings that have resulted from the traumatic experience.

For me, for example, the first time I did EMDR, we visited my feelings of shame.

Shame is a very common core emotion for folks with trauma, which is hard because it makes feeling any other emotion really hard. Shame is corrosive—it eats away at everything else until there's nothing left, and we just feel...empty.

And I'm no exception here. Shame has been a key theme throughout my mental pain over the years. So when I decided I was finally ready to start addressing some of my trauma for real, I found an amazing EMDR therapist, and we got to work.

Most EMDR therapists, mine included, don't just jump into EMDR exercises, by the way. You don't have to worry that you're going to get thrown into the deep end in your very first session.

First, my therapist and I built some rapport. We got to know each other, trusted each other a bit, had a few disagreements that we could work through in healthy ways, and more. I talked about my trauma a bit, in a very intellectualized "I'm totally absolutely fine with this now and don't need to feel any uncomfortable feelings at all" kind of way.

Then one day, I was really struggling, and my therapist asked if I'd like to try EMDR.

I was scared. I thought it wouldn't work, or I'd do it wrong, or I'd get triggered and feel worse, or who knows what else.

But I said yes. Because I'd been skirting around the issue of my trauma for years now. It was time.

She had me cross my arms and start slowly, gently tapping my shoulders, alternating left and right. Then she asked me to picture a safe space from the time of my trauma. A place where I felt slightly more comfortable being myself.

I pictured my childhood bedroom.

This room went through tons of redecorations over the years, but I pictured it from the Minnie Mouse era. Minnie Mouse wallpaper, Minnie Mouse bedding, even a Minnie Mouse lightswitch cover.

Then she asked me how old my inner child was, the version of me who was hurting right now. She told me not to overthink, just say the first age that came to mind.

I said she was six.

From there, my therapist guided me through the visualization of six-year-old me sitting on my bed, and adult me walking in and sitting with her.

Then she walked me through a conversation between these two parts of myself, and all the while, I was still gently tapping my shoulders back and forth.

And I realized my inner child didn't even realize she was being hurt. She wasn't mad about her trauma, like I am, because she didn't see it as trauma. She was in the process of internalizing all of it as her own fault.

As an adult, I just wanted to yell about how awful it was, what happened to us, but in the process of EMDR, I realized that's not what the six-year-old version of me needed. She needed to hear that she was a masterpiece of a person, and it was a shame that the people in her life didn't seem to see that.

So that's what I told her. And believe it or not, it soothed a lot of my pain.

And then, after some tears and more tapping on my shoulders, the therapist gently called me back to the current reality, and we debriefed. I didn't have to tell her everything I thought or experienced in the EMDR, but I felt free to tell her how it felt and generally what happened.

Then we finished our session and I unloaded the dishwasher and kept living my life.

It was weird, I won't lie. It felt like everything in my life should be radically different after such a powerful conversation within myself. But it wasn't.

Something I'm coming to learn after more than a decade of therapy is that I am always myself. There is no key or magic or anything that's going to turn me into a worthwhile person. I've always been worthwhile. The journey isn't taking me to a better version of me; it's taking me back to who I've always been.

EFT tapping

EFT stands for Emotional Freedom Techniques, and EFT tapping is a nervous system regulation tool that combines tapping various spots (mostly on your face) while also talking through difficult emotions.

Again, this might sound...very out there. Tapping your face and talking about your feelings is supposed to make you feel better? Seriously?

Well...yeah. Actually, both modern Western medicine[2] and Traditional Chinese Medicine[3] agree that EFT tapping is incredibly effective.

According to modern Western medicine, the spots you tap while doing EFT tapping help stimulate the parasympathetic nervous system, which is like the opposite of your fight or flight response. It encourages the body to slow down and relax into a sense of safety. Talking through difficult emotions while feeling safe can help us reckon with those emotions without getting overwhelmed by them.

According to Traditional Chinese Medicine, the spots you tap while doing EFT tapping are meridian points, areas where energy can get trapped in the body. And in Traditional Chinese Medicine, stagnant energy is often the source of illness and dysfunction. The tapping encourages the flow of energy, which in turn increases health and decreases illness, including anxiety, depression, and the effects of trauma.

Everyone does EFT tapping a little differently, but personally, I've developed a three-step system that seems to work pretty well for me and my clients.

Step one is acknowledgment. We just want to state our feelings, without judgment or shame. Or if we are ashamed, we just want to state that too.

For example, let's say I was working with a client who was feeling incredibly hurt after they had been left out of yet another social event by their so-called friends. We would start by tapping and saying out loud, "I am hurt. I am disappointed. I am confused. I am angry. I am sad," and whatever other emotions came up.

Step two is validation. It's important to make those emotions feel at home in our body, rather than unsafe or unwanted. This is the biggest piece that relates to inner child work, because oftentimes, as children, AuDHDers were taught that our emotions were too big, too much, dramatic, or just plain incorrect. So taking the time to say, "It makes sense that you're hurt. Your friends shouldn't treat you that way," can be so hard, but also so healing.

Finally, step three is a very gentle, very compassionate reframe on the situation. This is not going from "I'm hurt, I'm sad" to "I'm happy and fine!" If we're sticking with the friendship example, I might guide the client to say something like "Being left out absolutely sucks, and at the same time, I am glad I'm doing so much work on myself so that I'm good company for myself."

This three-step system allows you to feel your feelings without drowning in them, which is something I've been trying to do for, well, pretty much my whole life.

Journaling

I know, I know. Everyone and their brother tells you to journal, but you have ADHD, which means you buy the journal, write in it devotedly for three days, and then forget about it forever, right?

Yeah, same here. Except I don't think that's a bad thing.

See, journaling for three days gives you more insight than never journaling in the first place. This is the thing that we as ADHDers need to unlearn: something worth doing is worth doing inconsistently, irregularly, or even badly.

Temporary doesn't equal unimportant. Permanence is not a reasonable expectation for any human, let alone an ADHD human.

So journal for three days and then not at all for a month. Then journal again for two days, and not at all for six months. Then stick with it for a month before forgetting about it all over again.

It's okay. You are making progress this way. Your efforts are not wasted just because they aren't consistent. Consistency is not the end goal. The end goal is improving your life. If consistency gets you there, great, but if it doesn't?

Toss it.

EXERCISES

→ Identify the needs of your inner child, inner teen, and your current self, and explore how these needs are compatible or incompatible.

→ Split a paper in half. On one half write what your inner child wants to say, then on the other half respond as your current self.

→ Write down three unhelpful ways your caregivers responded to your AuDHD traits when you were a kid, then write down how you wish they had responded, then destroy the page to symbolize that no matter what we do, we cannot rewrite the past. We got the support we got, and all we can do now is change the future. To help you do that, write down how you can respond more helpfully to your own AuDHD traits, how you can be your own parent now.

KEY TAKEAWAY

→ You can't just push through your AuDHD and be the neurotypical person your caregivers or society may have expected you to be. You have to accept that you've been hurt, that hurt matters and requires healing in order to move forward as an AuDHDer.

CHAPTER 9

We Are Good Enough, Exactly As We Are

I'm going to tell you something so completely obvious and yet so completely radical that it might blow your mind a bit.

Ready?

Your brain is exactly the way it's supposed to be. You're not supposed to be neurotypical. You're supposed to be autistic and ADHD. The way you are is the way you're supposed to be.

Like...duh, right?

But also, how many times have you tried, relentlessly, to be neurotypical? To act neurotypical, to be perceived as neurotypical, to have neurotypical feelings and capabilities?

If you're anything like me, the answer is all the damn time.

I am a full-time AuDHD life coach, advocate, and content creator, and have been for several years now, and even I struggle to accept my brain the way that it is. I've grown very attached to and fond of my AuDHD label, but I'm still...less than fond of the actual traits sometimes.

And hey, that's fair. As we've discussed throughout this book, autism and ADHD can be debilitating, and you don't have to be thrilled about all your traits all the time.

But you don't have to love your autism and ADHD all day every day in order to love yourself all day every day.

The AuDHD identity: Separation and integration

You might read that sentence above, about not loving your AuDHD but still loving yourself, and feel...conflicted. I know I do. AuDHD is an integral part of who I am. There is no version of me that could ever exist who isn't autistic and ADHD. Any version of me without those things would be so radically different that she would simply be an entirely different person.

So how, exactly, can I not love my AuDHD, but still love myself? Aren't we one and the same?

Yes. And no.

Your AuDHD is an inextricable part of you. But it is not all of you. You have other aspects of yourself that could never be removed without changing who you are too.

For me, growing up middle class in the Midwest is like that. Had I grown up anywhere else, or even in the same place but with a different socioeconomic status, who I am would be completely different.

Having three amazing siblings is like that for me. If any of my siblings were different, or weren't born, I would cease to be the person I am today.

So there are many aspects of our identities, not just AuDHD. And sometimes, I fight with those amazing siblings. Sometimes, I resent the Midwest. But they're still part of me, and I can still love myself while being frustrated with them.

The same is true of AuDHD.

Some days, I really, really don't like being AuDHD. Just the other day, for example, my family and I went to a birthday party for my nephew. And I wanted to enjoy myself and have fun and chat with everyone, and instead, I was unbelievably overstimulated and went through a verbal shutdown for most of the party. Which, of course, I had to hide so I didn't make anyone uncomfortable or feel bad for me or bring up questions I wouldn't be able to answer anyway.

I wish that didn't happen. I'm very extroverted, I love parties and people, but sometimes my autistic brain just can't handle the things I like, and it shuts down.

And, oh boy, don't get me started on my ADHD. I love the energy and creativity it brings to my life, but I really, really hate the way it impacts my executive functioning. So often, like, nearly every day, there is something I know I need to do, something I want to do, even, and I just cannot. Because of ADHD. It loves building brick walls in between me and my goals.

And look, AuDHD is kind of my life. It's what I do all day, every day, and I have learned to accept so much about how my brain works. But here's the thing:

That doesn't change the way my brain works.

Self-acceptance can't cure AuDHD

Even if everyone in my life is accommodating and kind, even if I accept myself for who I am and feel absolutely no shame around my AuDHD, it still disables me.

I wish this wasn't true. I honestly thought it wasn't true for a long time, but alas, in my case at least, it is true.

Autism and ADHD are hard to cope with at times, regardless of how much personal support you have.

This is partially because no matter how supportive our personal bubbles are, our society at large is still very ableist and driven by oppressive systems like white supremacy and capitalism.

And even if those things disappeared overnight too, AuDHD would still disable me.

Let's say we live in a utopia where everyone is treated equally, accommodated, and has plenty of money to live full, rich lives. Wild, right?

And some of my friends and I decide we should go see a movie. We pick a showing and agree to meet at that time. I have plenty of money and time to see the movie, and I'm excited. My friends, knowing that I tend to perceive time differently, agree to text me several times before it's time to leave, so I don't miss the showing. Heck, maybe the movie theater even institutes some kind of reminder service you can opt into.

I sit on the couch and turn on some YouTube, with my phone right next to me. The "one hour until it's time to leave" text comes in and I see it, but keep watching YouTube, because I have a whole hour. Then the "15 minutes until it's time to leave" text comes and I see it, but keep watching YouTube because what am I going to do for 15 minutes if I turn it off now? Then the "TIME TO LEAVE" text comes, and I only have four minutes left in my video, so I finish it and get completely absorbed so that when it ends, I immediately click on the next video, keep watching, and totally miss the movie.

I had all the support in the world, but my perception of time and ability to regulate my attention are still very different from a non-ADHDer, and as a result, I end up missing something I was looking forward to, and maybe even hurting my friends' feelings, since they put in work to accommodate me, and I still missed it.

Should we look for a cure?

There are lots of reasons many AuDHDers oppose "cure rhetoric." Many people feel that the search for a cure is deeply rooted in eugenics, as discussed in Chapter 7, and in supporting Big Pharma more than supporting actual AuDHDers.

Even though I do take medication for my mental health, and it has been not only helpful, but literally life-saving for me, I also acknowledge that the pharmaceutical industry has a lot to gain from finding a cure, or even a treatment medication, specifically for autism.

As of right now, although there are some medications unofficially used to help reduce autistic agitation, the main "treatments" for autism are accommodations. And don't get me wrong, the pharmaceutical industry has really pushed for the use of those off-label medications in autism, and the wellness industry is making a pretty penny by simply adding the word "sensory-friendly" to regular items and charging 75 percent more for them, but imagine how much more money they could make if we had a cure for autism?

Personally, I would not take a cure for either autism or ADHD if one was discovered. As I said before, I feel like they are integral parts of who I am, and I am not interested in being a version of myself without them.

However, I know some AuDHDers who feel differently. Who see autism and ADHD as integral parts of them, yes, but integral parts that primarily make their lives harder, possibly even more dangerous, and they would very much like us to look for a cure.

So...should we look for one?

Here's my take: any cure that's rooted in getting rid of autism or ADHD because they are disruptive to society or inconvenient to people around the person with autism and/or ADHD is a bad idea.

All mental health treatment should be 100 percent consensual, and you cannot consent to something fully if you are being coerced. And an ableist society that makes it hard to love yourself, make money, or forge meaningful connections with others is coercing you into hating yourself and your disability.

As I said, I wouldn't personally take a cure, but I would also never stop someone else from taking it, as long as they were fully informed.

Here's something I've learned a lot about in the last year: autonomy is king.

Sure, I personally believe my autism and ADHD are disabilities, I believe they make me who I am, I believe if I'd been offered a cure as an emotionally tortured kid, I would have taken it and then missed out on this amazing person I am now, and I have concerns about how much money we put toward researching cures rather than researching the experiences of underrepresented people in our community, such as adult AuDHDers, Indigenous AuDHDers, AuDHDers in the global South, and so much more.

But at the end of the day, I cannot, and should not, ever tell another AuDHDer what to do with their life or their brain.

Dear reader, do what you want

If I'd read this book three years ago, it would have had the power to change my life, but I'm not sure if I would have let it.

Just a few years ago, I was starting to explore my brain and the possibility of autism and ADHD, but I was very wrapped up in the idea of getting everything "right." Basically, I thought I wasn't enough. Not good enough, not smart enough, not anything enough, and to make up for that, I had to be right about everything. It was my way of being safe.

I wouldn't have been ready to hear about autism and ADHD being disabilities yet. I wouldn't have been ready to talk about how the online AuDHD community often intentionally leaves out high support needs folks. And I definitely wouldn't have been ready to hear that some folks want a cure, and that's okay.

So if you're here, at the end of this book, and feeling a bit like you got hit by a freight train and you don't know what to think, I just want you to know, that's okay. This book isn't about being

AuDHD at work, or what it's like to get diagnosed, or how to be in a relationship when you're AuDHD.

It's about being a full AuDHD person, and all that it entails.

And I want you to do whatever you like with this information. Want to burn this book and forget you ever read it? Great. Want to post a 5-star review on Amazon and buy it for everyone you know at Christmas? Love it. Want to leave it on your shelf to gather dust and approach it again in a few years, with new lived experiences to help inform it the next time around? Sounds perfect.

Because here is the ultimate takeaway of this book:

You are in charge of you.

This doesn't mean you can magically wave away your limitations or overcome them with "growth mindset" or whatever.

It means you can do whatever the hell you want.

Seriously.

Anything. You can run headlong into the world of AuDHD, make it your job and personality and everything, like me, or you can appreciate it as a few meaningful brushstrokes in the masterpiece of who you are, or you can loathe it from now until the day you die.

Or something else.

It's literally up to you, and I support you, whatever you choose. I think there's a lot to love about being AuDHD, and I think it's part of my job to show that side of things to people, but I also think a key part of my job is to hold space for the parts of us that are hurting because of our AuDHD.

I really hope this book did that for you.

Thanks for reading, friend. And good luck on your journey.

Resources for AuDHDers

This book is largely about what to do next after realizing that you're autistic and ADHD, so obviously I had to include all the amazing resources I have been lucky enough to learn about and connect with over the years.

This chapter will cover three main resource types:

- helping professionals
- self-education resources
- content creators.

Let's dive in!

Helping professionals

Assessment/diagnostic support

- **Neuroclastic Directory of Diagnosticians:** This is a collection of assessors and diagnosticians who are specifically autism-affirming. It is a global directory, and many of the listings come with personal recommendations from people who have utilized their services. www.neuroclastic.com/diagnosticians

- **Embrace Autism:** This is an amazing education site, but the doctors who run it also offer assessments. www.embrace-autism.com/autism-assessments

- **GRASP:** Short for Global and Regional Autism Spectrum Partnership, GRASP offers assessments and coaching online. www.grasp.org/assessment-services

Therapy

- **Neurodivergent Therapists:** This is a collection of therapists who are neurodivergent themselves, and/or neurodivergent-affirming. It is a global directory, though listings outside of the United States, Canada, and the United Kingdom are limited. www.ndtherapists.com

- **Liberatory Wellness Network:** This is a directory for professional helpers of all kinds, from licensed mental health therapists, coaches, bodyworkers, doulas, Indigenous healers, somatic healers, herbalists, and more, who are all dedicated to anti-oppression, liberation, anti-colonial, and radical care. www.liberatorywellnessnetwork.com

- **Inclusive Therapists:** This is a directory a lot like Psychology Today, but better organized and more inclusive of a variety of lived experiences. This is a global directory, and you can search according to your location, but also according to your insurance, the specialty you'd like the therapist to be focused on, and more. www.inclusivetherapists.com

Coaching

- **Coaching with me:** As I mentioned in the book, I am an AuDHD life coach, meaning I love working with autistic, ADHD, and AuDHD folks (and people who are still exploring their neurotype). I specialize in executive dysfunction, emotional dysregulation, and internalized shame, and I do not work with sexual trauma or food trauma. Learn more, or set up a Zoom Discovery Call, on my website: www.theneurocuriosityclub.com

- **ADD Coach Academy:** I know I mentioned that outdated language, like ADD rather than ADHD, is a bit of a red flag for me, but I know several coaches certified through this program, and they're great, which is why I recommend searching the ADDCA directory for an ADHD-specific coach. Coaching is available in over 29 different languages, includes coaches from around the world, and you can also search according to the particular area you need help with, from relationships to college, and more. www.addca.com/adhd-coach-directory

- **Shimmer Care:** This is another ADHD-specific coaching resource where you can connect with a coach based on your answers to a quick quiz they have you take on their website. They orient their coaching around their concept of "Time, Done, Pause." www.shimmer.care

- **See also:** Many of the content creators listed below are also coaches. I will mention their coaching in the description of anyone who is also a coach.

Self-education resources

- **Autistica:** This is an amazing research and advocacy group based in the UK that helps autistic researchers get funding, while also educating autistic folks based on the research. You can learn more about autism, sign up to participate in research, and so much more on their website: www.autistica.org.uk

- **Embrace Autism:** As mentioned earlier in the Assessement/ Diagnosis portion, Embrace Autism does assessments, but they also have a super helpful blog, and an entire section dedicated to all kinds of free autism assessments you can take (with information on how accurate/reliable they are!). www.embrace-autism.com

- **University of Washington Autism Center:** This site is great for anyone looking to read lots of cool research about autism, though it's less good for folks who want things written out in layman's terms. www.depts.washington.edu/uwautism

- **CHADD:** If you're looking for an amazing and comprehensive introduction to ADHD, either for yourself, or for people in your life, CHADD's "About ADHD" overview is a great option. www.chadd.org/about-adhd/overview

- **Neurodivergent Insights:** Looking to learn more about neurodivergence in general, not just autism or just ADHD? You'll find tons of information here: www.neurodivergentinsights.com

Content creators

YouTube

- **The Neurocuriosity Club:** This is my channel! Come hang out with me! www.youtube.com/@theneurocuriosityclub *I am also a coach

- **The Thought Spot:** Irene is a thoughtful, engaging creator who posts all about her experiences with and thoughts about autism, and I highly recommend her channel! www.youtube.com/@thethoughtspot222 *This creator is also a coach

- **How to ADHD:** This is kind of *the* channel on YouTube about ADHD. Jessica and her team create funny, well-researched videos about all aspects of ADHD. www.youtube.com/@HowtoADHD

- **Yo Samdy Sam:** This is an amazing channel where Sam talks about her autism and ADHD and how they affect literally everything. www.youtube.com/@YoSamdySam *This creator is also a coach

- **Ami's Adventures:** Ami creates such unique content around his intersecting identities, but also around travel! www.youtube.com/@AmisAdventures

Instagram

- **Sonny Jane Wise (@livedexperienceeducator):** Sonny Jane Wise is an author, speaker, and so much more in the world of neurodivergence. They will teach you a kind of self-acceptance you probably didn't previously think possible. www.instagram.com/livedexperienceeducator

- **Laurel (@spectaculaurthoughts):** Laurel is a healer at heart, and her body of work will challenge everything you know about mental health, in the best way possible. www.instagram.com/spectaculaurthoughts *This creator is also a coach/helping professional

- **Lou (@neurodivergent_lou):** Lou's Instagram account is a veritable treasure trove of autism content and how autism can affect every aspect of our lives. www.instagram.com/neurodivergent_lou

- **Cate Osborne (@catieosaurus):** Cate is a certified sex educator who talks a lot about kink, consent, and the intersection between sex and disability. They're literally amazing. www.instagram.com/catieosaurus

- **Tiffany Hammond (@fidgets.and.fries):** Tiffany is an amazing autism advocate, plus a bestselling author, and I have learned so much from her Instagram account alone! www.instagram.com/fidgets.and.fries

References

CHAPTER 1

1   Cherry, K. (2023) 'Understanding habituation in psychology.' *Very Well Mind*. Accessed on 02/03/25 at www.verywellmind.com/what-is-habituation-2795233.

2   Kinnaird, E., Stewart, C., and Tchanturia, K. (2019) 'Investigating alexithymia in autism: A systematic review and meta-analysis.' *European Psychiatry* 55, 80–89. Accessed on 02/03/25 at www.cambridge.org/core/journals/european-psychiatry/article/investigating-alexithymia-in-autism-a-systematic-review-and-metaanalysis/06F8AA96D03679353022A52E6ACE2F50.

3   Aron, E. (2025) The Highly Sensitive Person. https://hsperson.com.

4   Mazefsky, C.A., Herrington, J., Siegel, M., Scarpa, A., Maddox, B.B., Scahill, L., and White, S.W. (2013) 'The role of emotion regulation in autism spectrum disorder.' *Journal of the American Academy of Child & Adolescent Psychiatry* 52, 7, 679–688. Accessed on 02/03/25 at www.sciencedirect.com/science/article/abs/pii/S0890856713003080.

5   Milne, E. and Smith, H. (2009) 'Reduced change blindness suggests enhanced attention to detail in individuals with autism.' *Journal of Child Psychology and Psychiatry* 50, 3, 300–306. Accessed on 02/03/25 at https://acamh.onlinelibrary.wiley.com/doi/abs/10.1111/j.1469-7610.2008.01957.x.

6   White-Gibson, Z. (2022) 'All about "autism meltdowns": Why they happen and how to cope.' *PsychCentral*. Accessed on 02/03/25 at https://psychcentral.com/autism/autism-meltdowns.

7   Stevens, K. (2019) 'Lived experience of shutdowns in adults with autism spectrum disorder.' Student Research Conference. Davis Center. University of Vermont. 17 April 2019. Accessed on 02/03/25 at https://scholarworks.uvm.edu/src/2019/program/91.

8   Pearson, A. and Rose, K. (2021) 'A conceptual analysis of autistic masking: Understanding the narrative of stigma and the illusion of choice.' *Autism in Adulthood* 3, 1, 52–60. Accessed on 02/03/25 at www.liebertpub.com/doi/abs/10.1089/aut.2020.0043.

9   Autistic Self-Advocacy Network (2017) 'Autism and safety toolkit: Research overview on autism and safety.' Accessed on 02/03/25 at www.autisticadvocacy.org/wp-content/uploads/2017/11/Autism-and-Safety-Pt-1.pdf.

10   DeLussey, S. (2023) 'The 8 executive functions.' *The Intentional IEP*. Accessed on 02/03/25 at www.theintentionaliep.com/executive-functions.

11   Price, D. (2021) *Laziness Does Not Exist*. Atria Books.

12   Micoulaud-Franchi, J.-A., Lopez, R., Cermolacce, M., Vaillant, F., Péri, P., et al. (2019) 'Sensory gating capacity and attentional function in adults with ADHD: A preliminary neurophysiological and neuropsychological study.' *Journal of Attention Disorders* 23, 10, 1199–1209. Accessed on 02/03/25 at www.journals.sagepub.com/doi/abs/10.1177/1087054716629716?journalCode=jada.

13   Williams, L.M., Hermens, D.F., Palmer, D., Kohn, M., et al. (2008) 'Misinterpreting emotional expressions in Attention-Deficit/Hyperactivity Disorder: Evidence for a neural marker and stimulant effects.' *Biological Psychiatry* 63, 10, 917–926. Accessed on 02/03/25 at www.sciencedirect.com/science/article/abs/pii/S0006322307011766.

14   Malkovsky, E., Merrifield, C., Goldberg, Y., et al. (2012) 'Exploring the relationship between boredom and sustained attention.' *Experimental Brain Research* 221, 59–67. Accessed on 02/03/2025 at www.link.springer.com/article/10.1007/s00221-012-3147-z.

15   Retz, W., Stieglitz, R.D., Corbisiero, S., Retz-Junginger, P., and Rösler, M. (2012) 'Emotional dysregulation in adult ADHD: What is the empirical evidence?' *Expert Review of Neurotherapeutics* 12, 10, 1241–1251. Accessed on 03/02/2025 at www.tandfonline.com/doi/abs/10.1586/ern.12.109.

16   Lloyd, D.R., Medina, D.J., Hawk, L.W., Fosco, W.D., and Richards, J.B. (2014) 'Habituation of reinforcer effectiveness.' *Frontiers in Integrative Neuroscience* 7. Accessed on 02/03/25 at www.frontiersin.org/articles/10.3389/fnint.2013.00107/full.

17   Hupfeld, K.E., Abagis, T.R., and Shah, P. (2019) 'Living "in the zone": Hyperfocus in adult ADHD.' *ADHD Attention Deficit Hyperactivity Disorder* 11, 191–208. Accessed on 02/03/25 at www.link.springer.com/article/10.1007/s12402-018-0272-y.

18   Kibby, M.Y., Vadnais, S.A., and Jagger-Rickels, A.C. (2019) 'Which components of processing speed are affected in ADHD subtypes?' *Child Neuropsychology* 25, 7. Accessed on 02/03/25 at www.tandfonline.com/doi/abs/10.1080/09297049.2018.1556625.

19   Gentile, J.P., Atiq, R., and Gillig, P.M. (2006) 'Adult ADHD: Diagnosis, differential diagnosis, and medication management.' *Psychiatry* 3, 8, 25–30. Accessed on 02/03/25 at www.ncbi.nlm.nih.gov/pmc/articles/PMC2957278.

20   Cepeda, N.J., Cepeda, M.L., and Kramer, A.F. (2000) 'Task switching and Attention Deficit Hyperactivity Disorder.' *Journal of Abnormal Child Psychology* 28, 213–226. Accessed on 02/03/25 at www.link.springer.com/article/10.1023/A:1005143419092.

21 Valko, L., Schneider, G., Doehnert, M., *et al.* (2010) 'Time processing in children and adults with ADHD.' *Journal of Neural Transmission* 117, 1213–1228. Accessed on 02/03/25 at www.link.springer.com/article/10.1007/s00702-010-0473-9.

22 Michaelis, J., McConnell, D., and Smither, J. (2012) 'Attention deficit/hyperactivity disorder's effects on individuals' scan paths during a simulated drive.' *Work* 41, 5833. Accessed on 02/03/25 at www.researchgate.net/publication/260435896_Attention_deficithyperactivity_disorder's_effects_on_individuals'_scan_paths_during_a_simulated_drive

23 Surman, C.B.H. (2012) *ADHD in Adults: A Practical Guide to Evaluation and Management.* 'Chapter 2: Clinical Assessment of ADHD in Adults.' Humana Press.

24 Koiler, R., Schimmel, A., Bakhshipour, E., Shewokis, P., and Getchell, N. (2022) 'The impact of fidget spinners on fine motor skills in individuals with and without ADHD: An exploratory analysis.' *Journal of Behavioral and Brain Science* 12, 82–101. Accessed on 02/03/25 at www.scirp.org/journal/paperinformation.aspx?paperid=116330.

25 Weyandt, L.L., Iwaszuk, W., Fulton, K., Ollerton, M., *et al.* (2003) 'The Internal Restlessness Scale: Performance of college students with and without ADHD. *Journal of Learning Disabilities* 36, 4, 382–389. Accessed on 02/03/25 at www.journals.sagepub.com/doi/abs/10.1177/00222194030360040801?journalCode=ldxa.

26 CDC (2024) 'Symptoms and diagnosis of ADHD.' Accessed on 03/25/25 at https://www.cdc.gov/adhd/diagnosis.

27 Surman, C.B.H. (2012) *ADHD in Adults: A Practical Guide to Evaluation and Management.* 'Chapter 2: Clinical Assessment of ADHD in Adults.' Humana Press.

28 Watson, N.F., Badr, M.S., Belenky, G., Bliwise, D.L., *et al.* (2015) 'Recommended amount of sleep for a healthy adult: A joint consensus statement of the American Academy of Sleep Medicine and Sleep Research Society.' *Journal of Clinical Sleep Medicine* 11, 6, 591–592. Accessed on 02/03/25 at www.jcsm.aasm.org/doi/full/10.5664/jcsm.4758.

29 Futenma, K., Takaesu, Y., Komada, Y., Shimura, A., *et al.* (2023) 'Delayed sleep-wake phase disorder and its related sleep behaviors in the young generation.' *Frontiers in Psychiatry* 14. Accessed on 02/03/25 at www.frontiersin.org/articles/10.3389/fpsyt.2023.1174719/full.

30 Neurodivergent Insights (n.d.) 'Bipolar vs. Autism.' Neurodivergent Insights. Accessed on 02/03/25 at www.neurodivergentinsights.com/misdiagnosis-monday/bipolar-and-autism.

31 Neurodivergent Insights (n.d.) 'Bipolar vs. ADHD.' Neurodivergent Insights. Accessed on 02/03/25 at www.neurodivergentinsights.com/misdiagnosis-monday/adhd-vs-bipolar.

32 Geissler, J., Romanos, M., Hegerl, U., *et al.* (2014) 'Hyperactivity and sensation seeking as autoregulatory attempts to stabilize brain arousal in ADHD and mania?' *ADHD Attention Deficit Hyperactivity Disorder* 6, 159–173. Accessed on 02/03/25 at www.link.springer.com/article/10.1007/s12402-014-0144-z.

33 Molina, B.S.G. and Pelham, W.E. (2014) 'Attention-Deficit/Hyperactivity Disorder and risk of substance use disorder: Developmental considerations, potential pathways, and opportunities for research.' *Annual Review of Clinical Psychology* 10, 607–639. Accessed on 02/03/25 at www.annualreviews.org/doi/abs/10.1146/annurev-clinpsy-032813-153722.

34 De Alwis, D., Agrawal, A., Reiersen, A.M., Constantino, J.N., Henders, A., Martin, N.G., and Lynskey, M.T. (2014) 'ADHD symptoms, autistic traits, and substance use and misuse in adult Australian twins.' *Journal of Studies on Alcohol and Drugs* 75, 2, 211–221. Accessed on 02/03/25 at www.jsad.com/doi/abs/10.15288/jsad.2014.75.211.

CHAPTER 2

1 Klassen, L.J., Katzmann, M.A., and Chokka, P. (2010) 'Adult ADHD and its co-morbidities, with a focus on bipolar disorder.' *Journal of Affective Disorders* 124, 1–2, 1–8. Accessed on 03/25/25 at www.sciencedirect.com/science/article/abs/pii/S0165032709003176.

2 Kondo, T. (2015) 'How and why is autism spectrum disorder misdiagnosed in adult patients?' *Mental Health in Family Medicine*. Accessed on 03/25/25 at www.researchgate.net/publication/308385920_How_and_Why_is_Autism_Spectrum_Disorder_Misdiagnosed_in_Adult_Patients_ _From_Diagnostic_Problem_to_Management_for_Adjustment_-.

3 Marschall, A. (2022) 'Who can diagnose autism in adults?' VeryWell Mind. Accessed on 02/04/25 at www.verywellmind.com/who-can-diagnose-autism-in-adults-6748943.

4 ADHD UK (2023) 'ADHD UK's report into NHS ADHD assessment waiting lists October 2023.' Accessed on 02/04/25 at www.adhduk.co.uk/nhs-adhd-assessments-waiting-lists-report.

5 University of Washington Autism Center (2023) 'Self-identification resources and communities.' Accessed on 02/04/25 at https://depts.washington.edu/uwautism/wp-content/uploads/2023/10/Self-Identified-Adult-Autism-Resources-handout-10.26.23.pdf.

6 Leitner, Y. (2014) 'The co-occurrence of autism and attention deficit hyperactivity disorder in children—what do we know?' *Frontiers in Human Neuroscience* 8, 268. Accessed on 02/04/25 at https://pmc.ncbi.nlm.nih.gov/articles/PMC4010758.

7 Milton, D.E.M. (2012) 'On the ontological status of autism: The "double empathy problem."' *Disability & Society* 27, 6, 883–887. Accessed on 02/04/25 at www.tandfonline.com/doi/abs/10.1080/09687599.2012.710008.

CHAPTER 3

1 Neurodivergent Insights (n.d.) 'The autistic and ADHD nervous system." Neurodivergent Insights. Accessed on 02/04/25 at www.neurodivergentinsights.com/blog/autistic-adhd-nervous-system.

2 Douglas, S. and Sedgewick, F. (2024) 'Experiences of interpersonal victimization and abuse among autistic people.' *Autism* 28, 7, 1732–1745. Accessed on 02/04/25 at www.journals.sagepub.com/doi/full/10.1177/13623613231205630.

3   Dodson, W. (2016) 'Emotional regulation and rejection sensitivity.' Accessed on 02/04/25 at https://d393uh8gb46l22.cloudfront.net/wp-content/uploads/2016/10/ATTN_10_16_EmotionalRegulation.pdf.

CHAPTER 4

1   My DisabilityJobs (2024) 'Autism and employment statistics—update 2024.' MyDisabilityJobs.com. Accessed on 02/05/25 at www.mydisabilityjobs.com/statistics/autism-employment.

2   My DisabilityJobs (2024) 'ADHD employment statistics—update 2024.' MyDisabilityJobs.com. Accessed on 03/25/25 at www.mydisabilityjobs.com/statistics/adhd-employment.

3   Lerner, D.A., Verheul, I., and Thurik, R. (2019) 'Entrepreneurship and attention deficit/hyperactivity disorder: A large-scale study involving the clinical condition of ADHD.' *Small Business Economics 53*, 381–392. Accessed on 03/25/25 at link.springer.com/article/10.1007/s11187-018-0061-1.

4   Our World in Data (2023) 'Unemployment rate in people with vs. without disability, 2023.' Our World in Data. Accessed on 03/25/25 at https://ourworldindata.org/grapher/unemployment-rate-by-disability?country=~USA

5   Kin, M. (2023) 'Entrepreneur statistics: Industry insights.' Markinblog. Accessed on 03/25/25 at www.markinblog.com/entrepreneur-statistics.

6   Embrace Autism (2018) 'Autistic brain differences: Connectivity.' Embrace Autism. Accessed on 02/05/25 at www.embrace-autism.com/autistic-brain-differences-connectivity.

7   Autistic Realms (n.d.) 'Monotropic interests and looping thoughts.' Autistic Realms. Accessed on 02/05/25 at www.autisticrealms.com/post/monotropic-interests-and-looping-thoughts.

8   Murray, D., Lesser, M., and Lawson W. (2005) 'Attention, monotropism and the diagnostic criteria for autism.' *Autism 9*, 2, 139–156. Accessed on 02/05/25 at www.journals.sagepub.com/doi/epdf/10.1177/1362361305051398.

CHAPTER 5

1   Social Security Administration (2024) 'Supplemental Security Income (SSI) Resources.' Accessed on 02/05/25 at www.ssa.gov/ssi/text-resources-ussi.htm.

2   *The Washington Post* (2024) 'Some disabled workers in the U.S. make pennies per hour. It's legal.' *The Washington Post*, August 30. Accessed on 02/05/25 at www.washingtonpost.com/wellness/2024/08/30/subminimum-wage-disabled-workers.

3   Hellman, R. (2018) 'How to make friends? Study reveals how many hours it takes.' The University of Kansas News. Accessed on 02/05/25 at www.news.ku.edu/news/article/2018/03/06/study-reveals-number-hours-it-takes-make-friend.

CHAPTER 6

1   Wise, S.J. (2019) 'What is neuronormativity?' Lived Experience Educator. Accessed on 05/02/25 at www.livedexperienceeducator.com/blog/whatisneuronormativity.

2   Brenan, M. (2020) 'Working moms get little reprieve from household demands.' Gallup. Accessed on 02/06/25 at news.gallup.com/poll/286739/working-moms-little-reprieve-household-demands.aspx.

3   Brenan, M. (2020) 'Working moms get little reprieve from household demands.' Gallup. Accessed on 02/06/25 at news.gallup.com/poll/286739/working-moms-little-reprieve-household-demands.aspx.

4   Ruderman Family Foundation (2016) 'Media coverage of law enforcement use of force and disability.' Ruderman Family Foundation. Accessed on 02/06/25 at www.rudermanfoundation.org/white_papers/media-coverage-of-law-enforcement-use-of-force-and-disability.

CHAPTER 7

1   Americans with Disabilities Act National Network (2023) 'How is disability defined in the Americans With Disabilities Act?' Americans with Disabilities Act National Network. Accessed on 02/06/25 at www.adata.org/factsheet/ada-definitions.

2   Disabled World (2025) 'Disabilities: Definition, types and models of disability.' Disabled World. Accessed on 02/06/25 at www.disabled-world.com/disability/types.

3   Michaelis, J.R., McConnell, D., and Smither, J. (2012) 'Attention deficit/hyperactivity disorder's effects on individuals' scan paths during a simulated drive.' *Work 41*. Accessed on 02/06/25 at www.researchgate.net/publication/260435896_Attention_deficithyperactivity_disorder's_effects_on_individuals'_scan_paths_during_a_simulated_drive

4   NPR (2020) 'ICE, a whistleblower and forced sterilization.' NPR. Accessed on 02/06/25 at www.npr.org/2020/09/18/914465793/ice-a-whistleblower-and-forced-sterilization.

5   Wise, S.J. (2023) 'Hidden disabilities or ignored disabilities?' Medium. Accessed on 02/06/25 at www.medium.com/@livedexperienceeducator/hidden-disabilities-or-ignored-disabilities-41e784ad87a.

CHAPTER 8

1   Butler, O., Herr, K., Willmund, G., Gallinat, J., Kühn, S., and Zimmermann, P. (2020) 'Trauma, treatment and Tetris: Video gaming increases hippocampal volume in male patients with combat-related posttraumatic stress disorder.' *Journal of Psychiatry & Neuroscience: JPN 45*, 4, 279–287. Accessed on 02/07/25 at www.ncbi.nlm.nih.gov/pmc/articles/PMC7828932.

2   Bach, D., Groesbeck, G., Stapleton, P., Sims, R., Blickheuser, K., and Church, D. (2019) 'Clinical EFT (Emotional Freedom Techniques) improves multiple physiological markers of health.' *Journal of Evidence-Based Integrative Medicine* 24, 2515690X18823691. Accessed on 02/10/25 at www.ncbi.nlm.nih.gov/pmc/articles/PMC6381429.

3   Wang, J., Yan, T.L., and Zhaoyu, D. (2024) 'The effect of Emotional Freedom Technique (EFT) on psychosomatic health: A Traditional Chinese Medicine (TCM) pilot study.' *Journal of CAM Research Progress* 3, 1, 116. Accessed on 02/10/25 at https://gexinonline.com/uploads/articles/article-jcrp-116.pdf.

RAISING READERS
Books Build Bright Futures

Dear Reader,

We'd love your attention for one more page to tell you about the crisis in children's reading, and what we can all do.

Studies have shown that reading for fun is the **single biggest predictor of a child's future life chances** – more than family circumstance, parents' educational background or income. It improves academic results, mental health, wealth, communication skills, ambition and happiness.[1]

The number of children reading for fun is in rapid decline. Young people have a lot of competition for their time. In 2024, 1 in 10 children and young people in the UK aged 5 to 18 did not own a single book at home.[2]

Hachette works extensively with schools, libraries and literacy charities, but here are some ways we can all raise more readers:

- Reading to children for just 10 minutes a day makes a difference
- Don't give up if children aren't regular readers – there will be books for them!
- Visit bookshops and libraries to get recommendations
- Encourage them to listen to audiobooks
- Support school libraries
- Give books as gifts

There's a lot more information about how to encourage children to read on our website: **www.RaisingReaders.co.uk**

Thank you for reading.

hachette
UK

---

1   National Literacy Trust, 'Book Ownership in 2024', November 2024, https://literacytrust.org.uk/research-services/research-reports/book-ownership-in-2024
2   OECD, '21st-Century Readers: Developing Literacy Skills in a Digital World', OECD Publishing, Paris, 2021, https://www.oecd.org/en/publications/21st-century-readers_a83d84cb-en.html